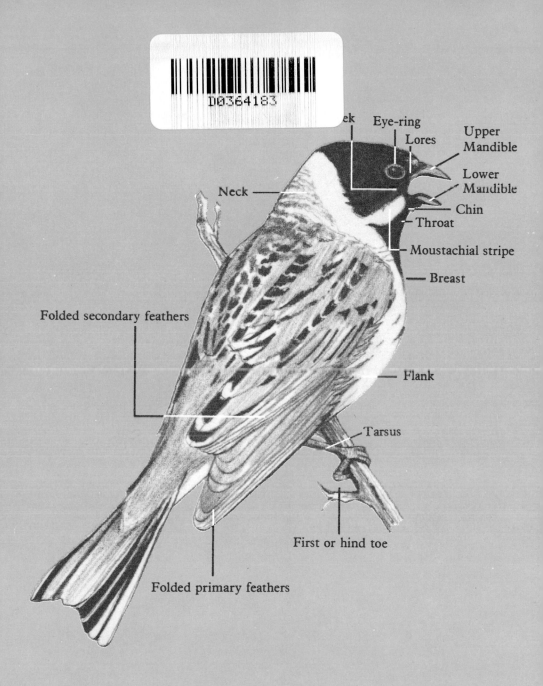

ek

Neck

Eye-ring

Lores

Upper Mandible

Lower Mandible

Chin

Throat

Moustachial stripe

Breast

Folded secondary feathers

Flank

Tarsus

First or hind toe

Folded primary feathers

Alan J Richards
BRITISH BIRDS
A Field Guide

David & Charles

Newton Abbot   London   North Pomfret (Vt)

To my wife Jenny

Acknowledgements

I am grateful to T.A. & D. Poyser, for allowing me to make use of the bird population figures given in their publication *The Atlas of Breeding Birds of Britain and Ireland*. Also to Malcolm Ogilvie, for the use of his *Birdwatchers Guide to the Wetlands of Britain* (B.T. Batsford Ltd) to ensure my wader and winter wildfowl figures were equally accurate. My thanks to Rob Hume, who not only drew the excellent line illustrations, but also cast his eagle eye over the text. Also I am indebted to my wife Jenny, who translated my almost unintelligible scrawl into something readable and then typed it again when I changed it. Without her help I doubt if the task would ever have been completed. Finally, I thank David & Charles Ltd for showing me such kindness and understanding during the preparation of this book.

Picture Credits

The colour illustrations are reproduced by kind permission of: T Andrewartha 52, 54; F V Blackburn 19, 43, 47, 49, 60, 102, 103, 107, 109, 112, 115, 145, 147, 148, 151, 153, 166, 181, 184, 190; J B Blossom 21, 25, 28, 36, 37, 38, 39, 40; A J Bond 14, 70, 71, 101; S C Brown 55, 120, 123, 144; A W Cundall 34, 85; G F Date 104, 155; R H Fisher 8, 69, 169; D Green 18, 44, 48, 64, 66, 78, 133, 134, 167, 182, 185; H A Hems 23, 135, 137; R A Hume 73; E A Janes 93, 94, 100, 119; E T Jones 187; R Kennedy 68, 74; H Kinloch 9, 15, 16, 51, 81, 86, 98, 121, 122, 127, 136, 141, 142, 143, 146, 154, 157, 174, 183; T Leach 170; W G McIlleron 10; A T Moffett 58, 114, 139, 161, 164, 168, 172, 173, 186; E Morgan 56; W S Paton 22, 33, 35, 42, 50, 61, 65, 87, 90, 108, 118; D Platt 45, 95; R Powley 178; M Richards (RSPB) 46, 156, 160; J L Roberts front cover, 11, 62, 67, 91, 92, 97, 105, 106, 116, 126, 132, 149, 150, 162, 177; B L Sage 83; R Siegal 41, 131; D A Smith 13, 17, 53; E Soothill 7, 26, 27, 29, 30, 32, 75, 76, 77, 79, 80, 82, 128, 140, 165; A F Taylor 72; E K Thompson 5, 6, 84, 89, 158; J Wagstaff 31; G W Ward 12, 88, 96, 125; P D V Weaving 180; M C Wilkes back cover, 20, 24, 57, 59, 99, 110, 111, 113, 117, 124, 129, 130, 138, 152, 159, 163, 171, 175, 176, 179, 188, 189; M B Withers 63

Introduction

This Guide has been produced for those thousands of people interested in the birds in their gardens and local parks, in the countryside or on the moors, by lakes or reservoirs. They need a short, clear Field Guide to identify the birds they see or are likely to see and to give a little background information about them.

The 186 species selected for full treatment here are those which might be seen in Britain without too much effort over the course of a year, though some limited travel is needed to locate a few with specialised habitat preferences; if you wish to see Crested Tit or Ptarmigan, for instance, it will be necessary to visit Scotland, and for a glimpse of a Bittern or a good view of a Bearded Tit, a trip to the RSPB reserves at Leighton Moss and Minsmere will greatly assist your chances.

The photographs have been chosen primarily to aid identification, though a further object in preparing this book has been to make it a pleasure to look at, and the skill of the photographers represented will be appreciated.

The marvellous thing about birdwatching is that it can be done anywhere, at any time; different places, different seasons, even different times of the day can mean different birds. It is not necessarily the wild and inaccessible places that provide the best birdwatching, either; in fact some of these areas, such as moorland, can be disappointing if it is numbers you are after. The coast invariably provides a great variety of birds; estuaries in autumn are particularly rich in wading birds, gulls and ducks, for example. Woodlands are best in late spring and early summer, and a lake or reservoir, especially if it has a muddy shoreline, can be interesting at any time. There are also many bird reserves throughout Britain: the RSPB alone has over seventy.

British Trust for Ornithology

The most authoritative scientific body concerned with ornithology in Britain today. Founded in 1932 to promote the scientific study of birds, especially among amateur birdwatchers, it organises many co-operative enquiries. A recent major undertaking was the 5-year survey of the breeding birds of Britain and Ireland 1968-1972, culminating in the publication of *The Atlas of Breeding Birds of Britain and Ireland*.

Royal Society for the Protection of Birds

Founded in 1889 as the Fur and Feather Group, at Didsbury, Manchester, to protest against the trade in birds' feathers for millinery, it soon widened its objectives and by 1891 had become the Society for the Protection of Birds. By 1897 the Society was also employing staff in London, and was granted a Royal Charter in 1904.

Today the RSPB is Britain's leading organisation concerned with the conservation and protection of birds and their habitats. Membership of the Society is continually increasing and is at present almost half a million. Details of the RSPB's activities and information on its many reserves can be obtained from The Lodge, Sandy, Bedfordshire SG19 2DL.

Some Birdwatchers' Terms
(For the parts of a bird, see labelled endpaper drawings)

Cock nest: a nest built by the male bird and not used. Typically applied to Wrens' nests not selected by the hen

Covey: a small flock or family group of Partridges

Crepuscular: active at twilight, eg owls or the Nightjar

Crustacea: a primitive class of mainly sea creatures, which includes water fleas, fish lice and shrimps, a principal food for many waders.

Diurnal: active by day

Feral: domesticated or escaped birds or animals now existing in the wild state

Hepatic: dark brown or liver coloured, eg a rare variety of Cuckoo (*Cuculus canorus*)

Hirundine: a member of the family *Hirundidae*, the Swallows, House Martins and Sand Martins

Irruption: a sudden invasion of a particular species occuring at irregular intervals, usually of birds from northern Europe, such as Waxwing or Crossbill.

Lek: a traditional site for the courtship ritual of certain birds, notably Black Grouse but also Capercaillie and Ruff

Molluscs: mainly hard-shelled marine creatures, a principal food of many wading birds

Nictitating membrane: the clear, third eyelid possessed by many birds and animals. Particularly obvious in the Dipper and used when the bird is under water

Nocturnal: active by night

Operation Seafarer: the name given to a survey of all coastal breeding seabirds in Great Britain and Ireland made in 1969-70

Passage migrant: a bird which passes through Britain during the course of its migratory movement, eg such wading birds as Knot and Bar-tailed Godwit

Pigeon's milk: a highly nutritious food manufactured in the crop of the adult Pigeon, with which the young are fed

Plucking post: a post or stump, or sometimes only a slight rise in the ground, where a bird of prey regularly dismembers its prey and removes feathers before eating. Usually easily recognisable by the remains scattered around

Race: a recognisable geographical sub-species

Roding: the Woodcock's display flight at evening, which follows a regular circuit over its territory

Sawbill: one of that group of diving ducks with narrow serrated bills, eg Goosander

Schedule I: The Protection of Birds Acts 1954 and 1967 in principle state that all wild birds, their nests and eggs, are protected. The Acts have four Schedules. Schedule I lists those birds, their nests, eggs and young, that are protected by special penalties. This Schedule includes all our rare or endangered species. It is an offence to disturb these birds at the nest, let alone take their eggs or young

Song flight: during courtship some birds indulge in particular types of flight whilst singing, eg the parachuting song flight of the Tree Pipit

Species: a population of birds that possess common characteristics. All members of that population or species are able to interbreed; members of different species normally do not

Sub species: usually a geographical population with some subtle differences in measurements, colour or song eg Pied Wagtail, White Wagtail

Summer visitor: a bird which spends the summer in Britain to raise its young, arriving in spring and departing in the autumn, eg warblers, hirundines

Winter visitor: a bird which spends the winter in Britain, usually arriving in the autumn and departing for its breeding area in the spring, eg wildfowl

Zygodactyl: having two toes facing forwards and two facing to the rear, as woodpeckers

Colour illustrations
Where appropriate the following symbols have been used:

♂ male   ♀ female   J juvenile   S summer plumage   W winter plumage

Red-throated Diver
Gavia stellata

Characteristics 21-23in (533-584mm). All divers have slender cigar-shaped bodies with legs at the rear, facilitating propulsion through the water where they spend most of their lives, only coming to land for nesting. The Red-throated is probably the most familiar of this highly aquatic group, having a slender uptilted bill which identifies it immediately, even at a distance. Only at close quarters can the dark red colour of the throat patch be seen. The head and neck are grey, the back an unpatterned grey-brown. In the winter it is a grey-looking bird with a whitish face, but at close range the back has a finely speckled appearance. It frequently dives to feed, mainly taking small fish, and often stays submerged for over a minute. If frightened it sinks like a submarine, the whole body awash, only head and neck above the water. In flight it has a long sagging neck, narrow wings and trailing feet.

Voice Noisy on the breeding grounds, having a mixture of wailing and mewing calls; also a short Crow-like warning call and a cackling flight note.

Habitat In the breeding season, it appears equally at home on large open stretches of water and on tiny lochans. In the winter, it frequents estuaries and coastal waters and is probably the most commonly noted diver on the sea. Infrequent on inland waters.

Nest Often no more than a scrape, usually within a yard (1m) of the water's edge, though it can be quite a heap of moss or aquatic vegetation with a small cup, built in shallow water. The 2 eggs are elongated and olive-brown, blotched with blackish-brown, laid May to June. One brood.

Status Present throughout the year. Breeding in N and W Scotland, also the Hebrides, Shetlands and Orkneys. There is a small population in Ireland. Probably less than 1,000 pairs in total. Afforded special protection under Schedule I of the Protection of Birds Acts, 1954 and 1967.

Winter plumage

5

Black-throated Diver
Gavia arctica

Characteristics 22-27in (559-686mm). About the same size as the Red-throated Diver, but its appearance in summer is quite distinctive, with grey head, black throat patch and black and white stripings on the neck. In the winter, however, it is basically dark on the upper-parts and white below, presenting a considerable identification problem, for it might be confused not only with the Red-throated but also with the Great Northern Diver (see later). Generally speaking, the Black-throated Diver looks much darker than *Gavia stellata,* has a straight, relatively slender bill and quite frequently shows a white blaze on the rear flanks. Its behaviour is much that of other divers. It submerges for long periods, often for half a minute or longer, during which time it travels a considerable distance underwater. Its food includes fish, crustacea, molluscs, etc.

Voice Highly vocal on its breeding grounds, producing a variety of sounds, including a croaking warning note which is frequently uttered in flight. It also has a number of distinctive wailing and whistling calls.

Habitat In the breeding season, similar to that of the Red-throated Diver but tending to prefer larger waters. As the Red-throated, it moves to estuaries and coastal waters in winter, but is more often seen on inland waters than the Red-throated.

Nest Usually a heap of vegetation with a distinct cup, sometimes in shallow water but more often on a small island. Less frequently, just a scrape. Eggs, normally 2, are greenish with some dark blotches, slightly glossy, laid in May. One brood.

Status Present throughout the year. Breeds in small numbers in the Outer Hebrides and Scottish islands, also parts of the NW Scottish mainland. Has become much scarcer in recent years, with total population probably no more than 150 pairs. A Schedule I bird.

Similar or Allied Species The Great Northern Diver *(Gavia immer),* largest of the divers, has nested in Scotland at least once, but is mainly a winter visitor. It might be confused with the Black-throated Diver; its angular-shaped head and massive bill should distinguish the two species, but from some distance away it is not always possible to be certain in winter. In summer the black head is distinctive.

(above) Great Northern Diver, winter plumage;
(below) Black-throated Diver, winter plumage

Little Grebe
Tachybaptus ruficollis　♂♀

Characteristics 10½in (267mm). The Little Grebe or Dabchick is the smallest member of the aquatic grebe family and very much a 'now you see it, now you don't' bird. It dives constantly and when not searching for its underwater food of amphibian larvae, small fish, etc, readily submerges at the slightest hint of danger, often seeming not to reappear because it re-emerges unseen in nearby reeds or water plants. Also when alarmed it may sometimes submerge until only its head is above water. When a protracted view is obtained the dark brown plumage of summer, with chestnut cheek, throat and foreneck is distinctive. Another distinguishing feature is the yellowish mark at the base of the bill; this is still diagnostic in the winter when the chestnut colouring of the face and throat are lost and it becomes a duller brown-and-buff looking bird. As all grebes, it is seldom seen on land, but it walks more easily than other members of the family. In autumn it collects in quite sizeable numbers, with 30 or 40 and sometimes more on suitable waters — constantly diving and reappearing, making counting difficult.

Voice A distinctive whinnying trill, likened to hysterical laughter. Regularly heard March to June, when male and female often trill to each other as part of their display.

Habitat Even the smallest pond will satisfy this bird's requirements as long as there is plenty of emergent vegetation, but it is equally at home on large lakes with plenty of cover. Slow-moving rivers, streams and canals are also favoured.

Nest This is entirely constructed of water weeds anchored to submerged vegetation. Often little more than a platform it can sometimes be a heap. The bird always covers the 4 to 6 dull white eggs before leaving the nest, a habit that tends to stain them a reddish-brown. The eggs are laid in April, though later clutches are common.

Status Present throughout the year. As a breeding bird generally distributed throughout England, but scarce or absent from parts of Wales and the SW. In Scotland less plentiful in northern areas and only a winter visitor to some places. Widespread in Ireland. Total breeding population is 10,000 to 20,000 birds. In the winter immigrant birds arrive from Europe.

Similar or Allied Species See Slavonian and Black-necked Grebes.

Winter plumage

Great Crested Grebe
Podiceps cristatus

Characteristics 19in (483mm). Our largest grebe, this very white-fronted bird with its long neck and pointed pinkish bill is a feature of many inland waters. In early spring, its weird head-shaking displays and the rarer weed-exchange ceremony may be witnessed. In summer plumage, both sexes have prominent chestnut and black frills on the side of the head which can be expanded and frequently feature in courtship rituals. These frills are lost in winter, when the birds have a dark-capped appearance with a white stripe over the eye. Nestlings are boldly striped black and white on the head and neck and frequently ride on a parent's back during their early life. The Great Crested Grebe swims with its body low in the water and neck erect; it dives to feed, taking mainly fish, though its diet also includes newts, tadpoles, etc, some vegetable matter and, as with most grebes, a number of feathers are eaten and also fed to the young. In flight it shows a double white wing bar, long thin wings and trailing legs.

Voice Usual calls uttered during the spring are a series of guttural far-reaching 'rah-rah-rah' notes and a long-drawn-out growling 'gorrr'.

Habitat In the breeding season, open water at least 2-3 acres (3-6 hectares) in extent with some emergent vegetation, particularly where fringed with reeds. In the winter, many resort to the sea coast and tidal estuaries, but are also found on large inland reservoirs.

Nest A platform of decaying weeds, typically on water but anchored to aquatic vegetation. The eggs, usually 3 to 4, are chalky white, becoming quickly stained, laid March or April. Sometimes two broods.

Status Present throughout the year, breeding widely in England with most centred in the Midlands and SE. Scarce or absent from SW England. Sparse in Wales and N England, does not breed in N Scotland. Breeds in Ireland though absent from most of the southern half. Total population probably around 5,000 pairs.

Similar or Allied Species The Red-necked Grebe *(Podiceps grisegena)* is a scarce winter visitor. It might be confused with *Podiceps cristatus* but is somewhat smaller, with dark neck, white face and yellow at the base of the bill.

(above) Great Crested Grebe, winter plumage;
(below) Red-necked Grebe, winter plumage

Slavonian Grebe
Podiceps auritus

Characteristics 13in (330mm). Somewhat smaller than the Great Crested Grebe but larger than the Little Grebe, this bird is as aquatic as other members of the *Podicepidae*. When seen in summer dress the glossy black head with a broad golden stripe through the eye is distinctive. These adornments look like small horns and give rise to its other name of Horned Grebe. Coupled with the brown back and chestnut neck and flanks, they distinguish it from the Black-necked Grebe, though in the winter both are basically black and white and can then present quite an identification problem. However, when the head pattern can be seen well, it is possible to distinguish between the two: in the Slavonian Grebe the black of the head comes down no further than the level of the eye, and the relatively stout and straight bill (not upturned as in the Black-necked Grebe) is a further clue. In flight it also shows less white than the Black-necked Grebe.

Voice A whinnying trill similar to Little Grebe, but also has a number of growling notes. Silent outside breeding season.

Habitat Small shallow lakes and pools, requiring less cover than the Little Grebe or Black-necked

Grebe. In winter, sheltered bays and estuaries. Also occurs in small numbers at inland waters.

Nest As other grebes, a heap of aquatic vegetation, usually anchored to submerged plants. Eggs, usually 4 to 5 laid in June, are oval and chalky white very soon stained brownish by nest material. Single brood.

Status Present throughout the year. A small Scottish population of around 50 to 60 pairs, with irregular scattered breeding records from other parts of Britain. A Schedule I bird.

Winter plumage

Black-necked Grebe
Podiceps nigricollis

Characteristics 12in (305mm). Similar in shape to the previous species, but is slightly smaller and in summer can be readily distinguished by the totally black neck, golden head plumes and uptilted bill. During winter, when both species appear basically black and white, there is much more of an identification problem. The Black-necked, however, has a black cap which extends well below the eye of the white face, and the uptilted bill is even more significant. In some young birds this may not be so marked and the face pattern is also less distinctive. It dives for its food, which is mainly fish though it also takes surface water-insects and eats feathers. Much shyer than the Slavonian Grebe at breeding sites, it generally keeps to cover during the day.

Voice Similar to the Slavonian Grebe's, but quieter and not so harsh.

Habitat In the breeding season, favours small shallow lakes with extensive reed beds or rich growth of other aquatic vegetation. Outside the breeding season, it moves to sheltered estuaries, also inland lakes and reservoirs where it is mainly noted from September to March.

Nest A floating heap of water weed anchored to aquatic vegetation. Often several nests are built before a final choice is made. The 3 to 4 eggs are chalky white, soon becoming stained by the nest material, laid late May to June. Sometimes two broods.

Status Present throughout the year, with a small Scottish breeding population of around 25 pairs. Has nested at other scattered localities in Britain and Ireland on occasions. Also a winter visitor in small numbers. A Schedule I bird.

Winter plumage

Fulmar
Fulmarus glacialis

Characteristics 18½in (470mm). A rather gull-like bird, but it is a member of the petrel family, having external tube-like nostrils which can usually be seen quite well as it patrols cliff nesting sites with effortless flight. Also its thick-necked appearance, and the narrow wings lacking black at the tips, should prevent confusion with any of the true gulls. Out at sea, it banks and glides on stiff wings just above the waves, recalling the Shearwater or Albatross, but flaps its wings more often. It often follows ships and occurs in large numbers at harbour landings or sewage outfalls, where it feeds on fish, fish offal, molluscs, crustacea and floating material of an oily nature. There are two forms of this bird: the usual light phase with head, neck and under-parts yellowish-white, upper-parts pearl grey with dark primaries and a pale patch near the tip of the wing, and a dark phase; but the so-called Blue Fulmar with its smoky-grey appearance is very rare in British waters.

Voice Noisy at nesting site, uttering a variety of cackling and grunting noises.

Habitat In the breeding season, coastal areas ranging from precipitous rocky stacks to low crumbling earth cliffs. At other times it occurs far out at sea.

Nest A cliff ledge, hollow or recess with no additional material added. It will sometimes use a coastal building. One white egg, with rough surface texture, laid in late May. One brood. At the nest the adult defends egg or young by spitting out an evil-smelling oily fluid.

Status Mainly a summer visitor, arriving at nesting sites early in the year, departing August to September. It has increased phenomenally this century. At one time its stronghold in Britain was the remote island of St Kilda, and before 1878 it nested nowhere else. Since then its expansion has been continuous and virtually every suitable site around Britain has been colonised or at least prospected. In 1969-70, Operation Seafarer estimated there were over 305,600 occupied sites in Britain and Ireland.

Manx Shearwater
Puffinus puffinus

Characteristics 14in (356mm). Most likely to be observed as it flies low over the sea with distinctive stiff-winged flight, alternating between periods of gliding and banking, the dark upper-parts and pale under-parts giving it a black and white appearance. During autumn migration it is often to be seen in continual procession as lines of birds cross the horizon. It is larger and longer-bodied than the petrels, with longer, narrower wings, and the bill is also longer and hooked at the tip, a feature which can only be appreciated at close quarters. Highly gregarious in the breeding season, it assembles in large numbers or 'rafts', settling on the sea at dusk near its nesting colonies. It returns to the nesting burrow in the dark, due to its vulnerability on land: it is heavily predated by the larger gulls. It swims quite freely when it feeds, taking food from the surface of the water, but it will also dive, catching small fish.

Voice Generally silent at sea. At nesting sites it produces a variety of raucous, crowing and crooning notes and typically a 'kuk-kuk-kuk-oo' call uttered in flight as well as in the burrow.

Habitat A maritime species, generally keeping to offshore waters during the breeding season, and it undertakes long oceanic flights to winter quarters.

Nest In an underground burrow excavated in soft ground, or in an old rabbit burrow. Nest chamber is lined with grass, roots, bracken, etc. One white egg, laid in May to mid-June. One brood.

Status A summer visitor, arriving February to March, leaving in August to October. Large colonies are mostly located on remote islands from the Shetlands down the W coast south to the Isles of Scilly. Some of the larger concentrations are to be found on Skokholm (35,000 pairs), Skomer (95,000 pairs) and Rhum (100,000 pairs). It also breeds at certain places round the Irish coast. Operation Seafarer estimated the total British and Irish population was almost certainly 175,000 pairs and could be over 300,000 pairs.

Storm Petrel

Hydrobates pelagicus

Characteristics 6in (152mm). Our smallest European sea bird, it resembles a House Martin with long black wings, white rump and squared black tail, though the under-parts are dark. Its flight, however, is not martin-like, as it flutters weakly just above the waves, pattering the surface briefly with its dangling black feet moving surprisingly fast, and taking fatty material, doubtless planktonic in origin. Frequently it follows in the wake of ships. It occasionally settles on the sea, floating buoyantly. Though active at sea during the day it returns to the nesting burrows at night. As other petrels, it has a characteristic musky smell, detectable at occupied nest sites. When annoyed it spits forth a smelly oil.

Voice It calls from the nest burrow with a harsh purring note ending with a distinctive guttural 'hiccough'. Silent at sea.

Habitat It feeds far out at sea, but frequents offshore waters during the breeding season. It occurs inland only when storm-driven.

Nest In a crevice amongst rocks and occasionally in peaty soil excavated by the bird itself, or in a rabbit burrow. Little or no nest material is added. The one egg is white with a few red-brown streaks at the large end, laid in June. One brood.

Status Recorded throughout the year, but is mainly a summer visitor, found from April or May to October or November. Most of the world's population nests in Britain and Ireland, with well over 50,000 pairs, mainly located along the western Irish coast. There are other major colonies on the Shetlands and on Skokholm.

Similar or Allied Species Leach's Storm Petrel *(Oceanodroma leucorrhoa)* is similar but a slightly larger bird, with a distinctive bounding flight. It is less numerous than the Storm Petrel. Major breeding places are the St Kilda group, the Flannan Islands, North Roma and Sula Sgeir.

(left) Storm Petrel; (right) Leach's Storm Petrel

13

Gannet
Sula bassana

Characteristics 36in (914mm). This large white sea bird with its long narrow wings tipped with black is identifiable at even the longest range — especially when typical feeding behaviour is witnessed, the bird diving for fish from 100ft (30m) or more up, sending up a shower of spray as it enters the water. Often many birds may be seen diving into the water one after another when a shoal of fish has been located. In fact size alone and the spear-shaped bill should be enough to put a name to the Gannet. In breeding plumage the adult bird's head and nape are yellowish-buff in colour. Young birds of the year are completely black-brown speckled with white, while sub-adults (it takes four years to assume full plumage) show a mixture of juvenile and adult plumage that might confuse the observer.

Voice Silent, except at breeding sites, when the chief note is a harsh 'urrah'. When uttered by several thousand birds at a colony this can be deafening.

Habitat Strictly marine, ranging far out at sea. In the breeding season, it frequents rocky islands with steep precipitous cliffs. Occasional storm-driven birds are noted inland.

Nest A large pile of seaweed, grass and feathers with a shallow cup lined with grass and other finer materials. A colonial nester, often many are together on cliff ledge or slope. The one egg is elliptical and translucent blue, becoming quickly stained, laid April to May. One brood.

Status Present throughout the year. British nesting Gannets (140,000 pairs) represent 70 per cent of the world's population. St Kilda alone has 60,000 pairs. Other well known colonies are on Bass Rock, with around 10,000 pairs, and Grassholm with 18,000 pairs. Bempton Cliffs, Yorkshire, is the only British mainland colony with around 100 pairs.

(left to right) Adult ; bird of the year ; sub-adult

Cormorant
Phalacrocorax carbo

Characteristics 36in (914mm). A large, dark, long-necked sea bird, often seen perched on buoys, posts or rocks, standing in typical heraldic pose drying its wings. In the summer, the bronze-brown or black upper-parts and bluish-black under-parts are offset by a white cheek and thigh patch, which the similar but smaller Shag does not have. The Cormorant's larger build and stouter bill should prevent confusion at all times, and with immature birds the more extensive whitish under-parts should also help to distinguish the two species. It flies low over the waves, often in small parties, line astern, the strong regular wing beats and outstretched neck being very reminiscent of geese. It swims low in the water, with head upward-inclined, and when alarmed will sink below the surface until only the head and neck are exposed. A voracious fish eater, this crow of the sea, as it is sometimes called, dives for its prey, invariably bringing its capture to the surface before swallowing it. Dives are irregular in duration, quite short compared with some fish-hunting birds, often less than half a minute. At sea, not a serious threat to commercial fish stocks; on inland lakes and rivers large numbers can be a problem, though they are as likely to eat perch and other coarse fish as salmon or trout.

Voice A low guttural croak rarely uttered at sea. At the nesting site, it has a varied and complex repertoire of deep guttural call notes.

Habitat In the breeding season, rocky coasts. At other times, may be met anywhere around our shores and quite frequently occurs far up tidal estuaries, also commonly inland during winter at some favoured localities.

Nest An untidy heap of seaweed, lined with grass. A colonial nester, with a partiality to cliff ledges and small rocky islets. There are a number of tree-nesting colonies in Ireland. The 3 to 4 eggs are oval, usually pale blue covered with a chalky white deposit, laid in April to May. One brood.

Status Present throughout the year, breeding mainly on western sea coasts of Britain and Ireland where suitable habitat exists. In 1969-70 Operation Seafarer found the total population to be just over 8,000 pairs, an important part of the European population.

Shag

Phalacrocorax aristotelis

Characteristics 30in (762mm). Closely resembling the Cormorant, its most distinctive feature is a short but conspicuous crest, though this is apparent only during the breeding season. At other times its small size and dark greenish-looking plumage (it is sometimes called the Green Cormorant) help to distinguish it. It also lacks the Cormorant's white cheek, and the hooked bill is less massive. The similarity of the two species carries over to their behaviour and food preference, but the Shag is more attached to rocky coastal areas and appears less inclined to perch on buoys and posts, etc, than the Cormorant. Immature birds are dark brown, showing little or no white on the breast, and their slender appearance and markedly slender bill — slenderer than the adult's — should prevent confusion with the larger birds.

Voice A series of clicking and grunting sounds made at the nest.

Habitat Exclusively marine, favouring rocky sea coasts. It is only rarely recorded inland.

Nest An untidy heap of seaweed and other available materials, lined with grass. A colonial nester, preferring ledges on sea cliffs, the nests often close together. The 3 to 4 eggs are oval, usually pale blue covered with a chalky white deposit, laid April onwards. Sometimes two broods.

Status Present throughout the year, being generally distributed along the Atlantic coast of Britain and Ireland, particularly on the Scottish W coast and western and northern islands. Virtually absent as a breeding bird from eastern coasts of England, southwards from the Farnes and westwards to the Isle of Wight. Operation Seafarer located 31,600 nesting pairs in 1969-70, of which 25,000 pairs were in Scotland, including 8,600 pairs in Shetland.

Bittern
Botaurus stellaris

Characteristics 30in (762mm). A shy secretive bird, it stalks through its reedy world on long green legs, the mottled, barred, brown and black plumage providing ideal protective colouring. If alarmed it assumes a 'frozen' posture with neck extended vertically, bill pointing skywards, making itself even more difficult to see. When taking one of its infrequent short flights from one reed bed to another, its heron-like appearance is more apparent, though its browner plumage and shorter neck immediately rule out the commoner bird. Most active in early morning and early evening it is then likely to be seen feeding, perhaps spearing eels in a marsh drain, for these are one of its favourite foods; however it will readily take any small aquatic creature, such as frog or water vole, also the young of other birds.

Voice The male's slow resonant booming 'er-whump' proclaims its presence in the spring. Though not all that loud, it has considerable carrying power and is audible up to one mile (1.6km) away. Both sexes also have a raucous 'aark-aark' note.

Habitat In the breeding season, marshy areas with tall emergent vegetation, especially reed beds. In the winter, wandering individuals might occur anywhere in Britain in suitable swampy or marshy places.

Nest A heap of dead vegetation lined with finer materials, situated in a dense reed bed. The 5 to 6 eggs are olive-brown, sometimes spotted at the large end, laid April to May. One brood.

Status Present throughout the year. Formerly more widespread. Most of Britain's 40-odd breeding pairs are now in Norfolk and Suffolk, though the RSPB reserve at Leighton Moss holds around 10 breeding pairs. A Schedule I bird.

Grey Heron
Ardea cinerea

Characteristics 36in (914mm). This large, long-legged bird with its dagger-like bill has a most distinctive flight silhouette which identifies it immediately. It flies with slow majestic flaps of its broad bowed wings, legs trailing behind, the long neck drawn back — not extended as the Spoonbill's. When perched it stands motionless for long periods in a hunched position, on a branch or rock or even in the middle of a field. When feeding it adopts a similar pose, but it often stalks through water with long deliberate strides, looking to spear any unsuspecting fish, frog or other aquatic creature. The Heron is particularly fond of eels, but its diet also includes water voles, mice, rats and young wildfowl. It is susceptible to severe weather and long periods of freezing weather create difficulties for it.

Voice A harsh 'fraank' frequently uttered on the wing. Very noisy at the nest.

Habitat Shallow fresh waters, marshes, estuaries, slow-moving rivers, canals, lakes and ponds.

Nest Most of the larger heronries that have been established over many years are well known. In Britain and Ireland these are invariably situated in trees. In Scotland, however, it often builds in low bushes and heather and on cliff tops. The nest itself is a bulky structure of sticks and is often the previous year's, repaired and added to. When in trees these nests often collapse under their own weight. A lining of finer materials is added for the 4 to 5 pale blue eggs which can be laid in early February if the weather is mild.

Status It has been studied annually since 1928 by the British Trust for Ornithology. Counts have shown a fluctuation from as low as 2,500 pairs (following the severe winter of 1962-3) to nearly 5,000 pairs more recently. However, many new heronries were discovered following field work for the BTO *Atlas* in 1969-72, and there are thought to be around 7,000 pairs now.

Similar or Allied Species The Purple Heron (*Ardea purpurea*), a darker, slenderer bird, with rufous neck and all-black crown. A rare visitor, mostly to E coast marshes.

Grey Heron

Mute Swan
Cygnus olor ♀

Characteristics 60in (1524mm). The commonest of the European swans — almost domesticated: some may even take food from the hand. Family parties, with their grey downy young, are typical of many a watery scene in late summer. The male or cob has all-white plumage and an orange bill with an enlarged knob; in the female or pen, the knob is much smaller. The male can be aggressive in the defence of its territory and will arch its wings and rush at any intruder, bird or human, hissing fiercely. In flight, swans are impressive; the loud mechanical throbbing of their wings is a most exhilarating sound. The young birds stay with their parents through to the following year, their plumage turning brownish and then white. White cygnets are uncommon and are referred to as Polish Swans. The swan feeds on water weed by dipping its head and neck below the surface of the water or by up-ending like a duck. It also grazes on meadows, flooded or dry.

Voice Not totally mute, in spite of its name, having a variety of snorting, grunting and hissing sounds.

Habitat It may occur anywhere, but in Britain is conditioned to living close to man, favouring canals, reservoirs, rivers, gravel pits, etc. It also frequents floodwaters, marshes and quiet coasts.

Nest A large mound of rushes, reeds and other vegetation, lined with some down, invariably near water, often on a small island. The 5 to 8 eggs are rounded at both ends, pale green, covered with a chalky deposit when laid. Egg-laying usually commences mid-March. Single-brooded, though it will lay a replacement clutch if the eggs are lost.

Status A resident, breeding throughout most of Britain and Ireland apart from the unsuitable upland areas. Total population is around 6,000 pairs.

Similar or Allied Species Two species of truly wild swans which occur in Britain might be confused with the Mute Swan. These are the Bewick's Swan *(Cygnus bewickii)* and Whooper Swan *(Cygnus cygnus)*. These two species are generally less approachable and invariably look more alert, holding the neck erect rather than in the graceful S-bend of the Mute Swan. The Bewick's Swan is slightly smaller than the Mute, the Whooper the same size. The best distinguishing feature, however, is the bill, patterned black and yellow (see drawing). Bewick's and Whooper are both winter visitors. The former species is regular in considerable numbers at Slimbridge, Gloucestershire (around 400), and the Ouse Washes (up to 1200). Smaller herds are frequent at inland waters, on floodland and at coastal sites. The Whooper Swan is much more unusual outside Scotland and Wales, where most of the birds (about 3,500) are to be found from October to April.

(above, left to right) Mute Swan, Whooper Swan, Bewick's Swan; (below, left) Mute Swan (right) Bewick's Swan

19

Pink-footed Goose

Anser brachyrhynchus

Characteristics 24-30in (610-762mm). A medium-sized goose with a short black bill with a pink band, pink legs. Smaller than the commoner Greylag, a distinctive feature is undoubtedly the contrast between the dark head and lighter-coloured body, which provides a more or less immediate means of identification. In flight the forewing is noticeably pale greyish, though not as pale as the Greylag's. A highly gregarious species, the Pink-footed Goose feeds and roosts in large flocks. Though a shy bird, it favours farmland, where it feeds on stubble and in potato fields. It is tolerant of other species, and mixed flocks can be found together, though Pink-feet tend to feed separately. It flights daily between roosting and feeding grounds, spending the night on sandbanks of coasts and estuaries or on marshes where not disturbed.

Voice Usual call is a disyllabic 'ung-unk', which is not as deep as the Greylag's or as high-pitched as that of the White-fronted Goose. It has a high-pitched alarm squeal, and also a distinctive 'wink-wink'.

Habitat Grassland and arable fields near coasts, marshes and estuaries.

Status A winter visitor. Birds that breed in Iceland and Greenland arrive in Britain around the end of August or early September, staying until April or May. Most are to be found in Scotland, but increasing numbers occur in the Southport area and some smaller flocks around the Wash. Total winter population around 75,000 birds.

Similar or Allied Species The Bean Goose *(Anser fabalis)* is slightly larger and the bill is longer and black, marked with orange and yellow, occasionally with some white feathers at its base. The forewing is dark, which rules out Greylag or Pink-footed Goose, and legs orange. It has declined as a winter visitor to Britain, and is now quite scarce with probably no more than 200 birds all told. Most regularly to be found in Norfolk and Galloway (Scotland).

Pink-footed Goose

White-fronted Goose
Anser albifrons

Characteristics 26-30in (660-762mm). Somewhat smaller and darker-looking than the Greylag, the adult can be distinguished from other 'grey geese' by a bold white patch above the pink bill, orange legs and broad irregular black bars on the belly. These bars may be very slight or make the belly almost completely black. The sexes are similar though the male is slightly larger. Immature birds lack both the white forehead and the black barring on the breast, and when not with adults identification could be a problem; but the combination of orange legs and lack of extensive black on the bill are distinctive. Slimmer-winged and quicker in flight than most other grey geese, the White-fronted also lacks the very pale forewing typical of Greylag and Pinkfoot. Grass is the main diet, taken by a rapid pecking motion as the bird walks.

Voice Characteristic and unmistakable, being higher-pitched than those of other grey geese, and with a laughing quality, giving rise to the name Laughing Goose in some areas.

Habitat Grasslands, wet pastures and saltings.

Status A winter visitor, arriving October to November, departing from February to April or May. In recent years numbers have declined in Britain at the expense of preferred Dutch feeding grounds. The Severn estuary wintering flock, centred on the Wildfowl Trust's headquarters at Slimbridge, is probably the best known in England. The total wintering in England has declined to approximately 6,000 birds.

Similar or Allied Species There is a darker orange-billed race breeding in Greenland, with around 4,000 birds wintering in Scotland, Ireland and Wales. The similar but smaller Lesser White-fronted Goose (*Anser erythropus*) is a rare visitor, with one or two recorded annually. It has a larger amount of white and a yellow ring around the eye.

White-fronted Geese: (left) juvenile (right) adult

Greylag
Anser anser

Characteristics 30-35in (762-889mm). All grey geese resemble the domestic goose. This species, particularly, is the ancestor of the familiar farmyard bird. The largest and heaviest goose, it makes an impressive sight as it flies to and from the feeding grounds to graze for most of the day in grass fields or marshes. Prior to landing the geese often perform striking aerobatic movements, plunging downwards in side-slipping, rolling erratic dives known as whiffling. The Greylag has the palest forewing of all the geese, a useful identifying feature. The bill is bright orange and the legs and feet are flesh-pink. The term 'lag' is a contraction of 'laggard', for this species stays behind when others migrate from British shores.

Voice A loud 'aahng-ung-ung' just like the farmyard bird. When heard in large flocks Greylags can sound like a pack of hounds in full cry.

Habitat In the breeding season feral birds are found on large stretches of open water such as the Norfolk Broads, large reservoirs and gravel pits. Naturally breeding birds are very local, favouring moorland with small lochans or the vicinity of larger lochs and small offshore islands. In the winter, grassland, arable fields near coastal marshes and estuaries.

Nest A hollow, lined with locally available material, heather, moss, grass, rushes, etc, some feathers and down, situated in vegetation, often close to the water. The 4 to 6 eggs are creamy-white, often stained yellowish-brown, laid from mid-March but usually April to May. One brood.

Status Most birds breeding in Britain are feral, the wild population having been almost eliminated over the last 200 years. Probably only about 200 pairs of truly wild birds are now nesting in Scotland. Around 600-800 pairs of feral birds are scattered throughout the UK, with notable concentrations in County Down, Kent, Norfolk and the Lake District. In the winter some 65,000 birds from Iceland join the resident population, mostly in mid-Scotland.

Canada Goose
Branta canadensis   ♀ ♂

Characteristics 36-40in (911-1016mm). Distinguished from other black geese by its long black neck and head with a broad white throat and cheek patch contrasting with a white breast and brown body. The largest of the geese occurring in Europe, much bigger than the Barnacle Goose which to some extent it resembles in face pattern. It swims frequently when it feeds on aquatic plants by dipping its head into the water and sometimes by up-ending. Also spends long periods grazing on grass and occasionally on growing crops. It flies fast with deep regular wing beats in either loose flocks, V formation, diagonals or single file. It whiffles on landing when coming in to roost.

Voice A variety of deep resonant honking calls.

Habitat Fresh water lakes, reservoirs, sand and gravel pits, but also fields and open marshes. Ornamental lakes in parkland with surrounding trees — its original habitat in Britain is still a stronghold for this bird. Sometimes found on the sea and estuaries.

Nest A hollow in the ground lined with grass, reeds, dead leaves, etc, and down. Generally close to the water, often on a small island. The 5 to 6 eggs are dull white to creamy white, laid in April to May. One brood.

Status Present throughout the year. This species was brought to Britain as an ornamental bird during the reign of Charles I and by the end of the eighteenth century was breeding freely in the wild. The first national census, organised by the British Trust for Ornithology in 1953, found around 3,500 birds to be present. By 1967-9 the Wildfowl Trust Survey found the total had risen to about 10,000 pairs. The species is still increasing with the original sub-population of a non-migratory feral race gradually becoming less distinct. But still relatively scarce in Scotland and Wales and only a few in Northern Ireland.

23

Barnacle Goose
Branta leucopsis

Characteristics 23-27in (584-686mm). This species is usually more approachable than other geese, but is readily identified even at long range by its combination of black, white and grey, the white face contrasting with the black crown and breast while the bill is short and stubby, especially when compared with grey geese. Highly gregarious as are all geese, Barnacle Geese do, however, tend to keep to their own kind, rarely mixing with other geese, perhaps because they are a quarrelsome species and much bickering goes on in the flock. They feed on grass, grazing in the usual manner during the day, flighting to and from roosts on tidal flats at dusk and dawn. They will continue to feed at night when the moon is full.

Voice A noisy bird, generally, and the continual calling of a flock has been likened to the sound of small dogs yapping. The individual call, however, is a shrill monosyllabic bark.

Habitat More terrestrial than the Brent Goose, preferring the rich turf of coastal meadows and saltings, rarely settling on the sea. Occasionally it is to be found on cultivated land.

Status A winter visitor to Britain, arriving September to October and departing April to May. Birds which breed in Greenland winter in W Scotland and Ireland; the most important centre for this group is the island of Islay in the Inner Hebrides, where over 20,000 birds occur. Birds which breed in Spitzbergen, winter only on the Solway round to the Caerlaverock area, where, due to protection, a population of a few hundred has now been increased to over 6,000 birds. The other major wintering zone is the Netherlands, where the remaining 50,000 of the world's population of this species is to be found. The Barnacle Goose is only occasionally noted in other parts of Britain, and individual birds seen at unusual times of year could well have escaped from wildfowl collections.

Brent Goose
Branta bernicla

Characteristics 22-24in (559-610mm). Smallest and darkest of the black geese (little larger than a Mallard), adults have the entire head, neck and upper breast black, with variable white markings forming a partial or sometimes almost complete collar round the neck. The stern is a brilliant white which shows as a distinctive V when flying. Flight is swift, usually in irregular lines or packs, fairly low over the sea, gracefully writhing and undulating. More maritime than other geese, it is virtually confined to the intertidal zone, to feed on its staple diet of eel grass (*Zostera*) which grows in shallow muddy coastal areas between high and low water marks. It feeds day and night, up-ending more frequently than other geese. As the population has increased in recent years flocks have begun to feed in coastal fields.

Voice A guttural honking 'krronk'.

Habitat Tidal flats and estuaries where *Zostera* is found.

Status A winter visitor to Britain, breeding in the high Arctic. The birds usually arrive in October, departing March to April. Two distinct races are identifiable. The pale-bellied race from Canada, Greenland and Spitzbergen, winters on the eastern seaboard of the USA, and also in Europe at a few localities on the North Sea coasts and parts of Ireland. The dark-bellied race is the more numerous in Europe, and major areas where it occurs in Britain include the Exe Estuary, Essex marshes and North Norfolk. In the mid-1950s the total world population was only around 11,000 birds, but it is now one of the commonest geese in NW Europe, with a total population probably around 150,000 birds, about a quarter of this number visiting Britain.

R.AH.

25

contrasting plumage comprises a greenish-black head and neck, with a broad chestnut band around the forepart of the white body. There is also a dark stripe down the centre of the underparts and black bands on the upper-parts. The legs are pink and the bill is red, the male's having a prominent knob. Juvenile birds look quite different, having no breast band or belly stripe, a pink bill and grey legs. It walks easily over mud banks and sandflats, where it feeds on molluscs, crustaceans or worms. When swimming it sits quite high in the water; it might be confused with the Shoveler when sieving for food, but its size alone should distinguish it.

Voice The male has a low whistling note and the female a distinct 'gah-gah-gah' call, uttered in flight and when at rest.

Habitat A coastal bird, favouring sandy and muddy areas with sand dunes or salt marshes, but it also occurs quite far inland on fresh water.

Nest Composed mostly of down, usually in a rabbit burrow or underground cavity; it also commonly tunnels under brambles, gorse, bracken or heather. The eggs, 8 to 10, are creamy white, laid in April to May. One brood.

Status Present throughout the year and found round most of coastal Britain and Ireland. Having increased considerably as a breeding bird in recent years, it is also colonising inland areas, particularly the Ouse Washes. The breeding population is probably around 12,000 pairs, and the total population, which includes many non-breeding birds, is probably twice this number.

(left) Female; (right) male

Shelduck
Tadorna tadorna   ♂

Characteristics 24in (610mm). When seen in flight this goose-like bird looks very black and white, hence the name Sheld-duck which means pied-duck (no connection with a shield). Close to, however, it will be seen that the boldly

Wigeon
Anas penelope ♂

Characteristics 18in (457mm). The male is distinguished by its chestnut-coloured head with yellow forehead, grey body and pinkish breast. Somewhat smaller than the Mallard, the head is rounder looking and the bill much smaller. The duck, though less colourful, is rufous-looking and with its small bill and a pointed tail should be quite easily identified. In flight, the broad white patches towards the front of the wing and the white under-parts, contrasting with the black, are distinctive features of the drake. Though it feeds from the surface of the water, it obtains much of its food by grazing and flocks of Wigeon may be seen obtaining their food in this way.

Voice The drake has a long musical whistle, 'whee-oo'. The duck has a purring note and a harsh growling alarm call.

Habitat In the breeding season it favours lakes, pools and streams on open moorlands and in cultivated or wooded country. In the winter it is found along coasts, estuaries and salt marshes; also inland on large lakes and reservoirs.

Nest A shallow depression on the ground, lined with grass and leaves. Usually well concealed it is invariably near the water. Down is added after the 6 to 10 creamy white eggs are laid in May. One brood.

Status Present throughout the year. As a breeding bird it first colonised Britain in the nineteenth century, nesting in Sutherland. Most records still come from Scotland, though there are scattered occurrences in northern England and East Anglia. Probably up to 500 pairs nest. It does not breed in Ireland. It is a common winter visitor from Scandinavia and Arctic Russia, with an estimated 200,000 present from October to March.

(left) Female; (right) male

Gadwall
Anas strepera ♂

Characteristics 13in (330mm). When observed sitting out on a lake or reservoir, even the male bird can be mistaken for a female Mallard. However, close scrutiny shows it to be slightly smaller, generally greyer-looking, with a black rear end. A really close look reveals that the head and neck are brown, speckled with dark markings, the back and flanks finely vermiculated with grey. At rest the white speculum, the bright area of wing feathers possessed by all surface-feeding ducks, is not always obvious, but in flight it is most distinctive, showing as a white patch on the hind border of the wing; the pale belly contrasting with the black rear is also a noticeable feature. The female is much like a female Mallard but the white speculum immediately identifies her if it is visible; however, as in the male, this is often concealed when at rest. Additionally, an orange line along the bill is a good distinguishing feature and the orange-yellow legs (not orange-red) will be seen when the bird up-ends. From May to September the male assumes eclipse plumage and looks very much like the female. As other surface feeders, it dabbles for vegetable matter, chiefly seeds and roots of aquatic plants, and a quantity of animal food is also taken.

Voice The male has a chuckling croak, while the female utters a coarser Mallard-like 'quack'.

Habitat In the breeding season, quiet lakes, marsh pools and other still waters with good cover, or sluggish running water bordered by rank vegetation. In the winter, lakes, reservoirs, marshes and occasionally on the sea.

Nest Down is mixed with grasses and other vegetation, on the ground in thick vegetation close to the water. The 8 to 12 eggs are creamy buff, laid in May or early June. One brood.

Status Present throughout the year, breeding at scattered localities in Britain with most concentrated in Norfolk and Suffolk. Only a few pairs regularly nest in Ireland. The total population is probably around 250 pairs. Wintering birds from the Continent arrive between August and October, leaving in March and April. Probably now more than 2,000 to 3,000 birds in all.

Teal
Anas crecca ♂

Characteristics 14in (356mm). When observed at a distance this gives the impression of being a small grey bird with a dark head — it is in fact our smallest duck. At rest, the drake shows a noticeable long white line on the closed wing, while creamy-white triangular patches at its rear are distinctive. Quite a colourful bird when seen close to, it has a chestnut-brown head with a broad band of metallic green outlined with buff enclosing the eye and extending to the nape. The back and flanks are finely pencilled with grey, while the breast is heavily spotted and the under-parts are white. The female is mottled brown and buff, paler and spotted below, but often shows the distinctive speculum which is half metallic green and half black. When disturbed from the water it will leap almost vertically into the air to take off, hence the term used by sportsmen 'a spring of teal'. The flight is fast and when in flocks it wheels and turns erratically, similar to a group of waders, first showing the darker upper-parts, then lighter under-parts. A surface feeder, it sieves and dabbles for food, basically vegetable matter.

Voice The male has a musical 'krit-krit' call. The duck utters a short sharp 'quack', usually when alarmed.

Habitat In the breeding season, rushy moorland and heath pools of upland areas but also lowland marshy areas, lakes and stream sides where plenty of cover exists. At other times, reservoirs, lakes, rivers, floodwater, estuaries and salt marshes. Occasionally on the sea.

Nest A hollow or scrape, lined with leaves, grass and other vegetation, also a large amount of down. Usually in thick vegetation near water. The 4 to 8 eggs are smooth and yellowish-white, laid April to May. One brood.

Status Present throughout the year and commonest as a breeding bird in Scotland (except NW) and northern England. Smaller numbers nest in East Anglia and SE England. Sporadic in the Midlands, and a few records from the SW. Scattered breeding in Wales. Widely but thinly distributed in Ireland, except in the SW. Total breeding population probably around 5,000 pairs. Winter visitors swell the mainly sedentary breeding population to around 75,000 birds.

Similar or Allied Species The Garganey (*Anas querquedula*) is only slightly larger than the Teal. Drakes have a distinctive broad white band extending from the eye to the nape. A summer visitor, but a few pairs nest each year.

Male Teal

Mallard
Anas platyrhynchos ♂

Characteristics 23in (584mm). Most familiar of all our wildfowl, the drake Mallard or Wild duck is a handsome and colourful bird with its bottle-green head, yellow bill, white collar, grey back and flanks, distinctive curly black tail feathers and orange-red legs. As with all members of the *Anatidae* (duck family), the female lacks the drake's bright plumage and is a mixture of browns, blacks and buff, an obvious advantage when sitting on a nest — most ducks being ground-nesters and vulnerable to predators. In the Mallard the speculum, the bright wing-patch seen in flight, is purple, bordered each side with black and white. Both male and female have this distinctive feature. All drakes moult their breeding dress towards the end of summer and assume eclipse plumage, then resembling the female. For a short period during this change they are flightless. The Mallard, as other surface feeders, sifts shallow water with its bill which has a sieve-like mechanism, called lamellae, so that small animal and vegetable matter can be extracted. It does, however, also feed on land, grazing or picking up worms, snails, slugs, etc.

Voice Most of the quacking associated with this bird comes from the female, the drake only making a rather weak nasal 'neb'.

Habitat Virtually any type of water situation, from large lakes and reservoirs to small ponds, canals and slow rivers. It is also found on estuaries, salt marshes and the sea. Extremely tolerant of humans, it readily visits park lakes even in city centres, where it quickly becomes quite tame.

Nest Grass and dead leaves plus a lining of down, usually a short distance from the water in thick undergrowth, but often in woodland or hedgerows. It soon takes to artificial nest sites such as duck baskets. The 8 to 9 (often up to 12) eggs are grey-green or buff-coloured, often laid as early as March. Larger clutches are usually the result of two females laying in one nest. One brood.

Status The most numerous and widely distributed of our resident waterfowl, nesting throughout the whole of Britain and Ireland. The total population is certainly over 70,000 pairs and could well be as high as 150,000 pairs. Most of the British population is sedentary, and is supplemented by winter visitors from N Europe, which could bring the total to over half a million birds.

(left) Female ; (right) male

30

Pintail

Anas acuta   ♂♀

Characteristics 22in (559mm). A slender-necked duck with long central tail feathers, this surface feeder is a most attractive and elegant bird. The drake has a chocolate-brown head with a white stripe running down the neck extending to a white breast and under-parts. It sits high on the water, its tail elevated, generally keeping its distance from the observer. The female's tail is shorter and her brown plumage is paler and more finely speckled than the Mallard duck's. The slender grey bill is also a useful distinguishing feature. It flies with rapid wing beats and then the white trailing edge of the wing is seen. It feeds mainly at night, on a wide variety of animal and vegetable matter.

Voice As a rule a quiet bird, but occasionally it utters some Mallard-like quacks.

Habitat In the breeding season, open shallow waters, fresh water marshes and floodlands. During the winter it is found chiefly on estuaries and sea coasts, but occasionally in small numbers inland on large lakes and reservoirs.

Nest A slight hollow usually lined with grass and leaves, sometimes not, though always lined with down. Normally it is in short grass but often it is quite exposed. The 7 to 10 eggs are usually yellowish-green, laid in May. One brood.

Status First recorded nesting in Scotland in 1869. The present breeding population of around 50 pairs is scattered about Britain, with most in Scotland and Northern England. It also nests regularly on the Ouse Washes and N Kent marshes, and occasionally in Ireland. In the winter, concentrations of immigrant Pintail are to be found on the estuaries of NW England, while the Ouse Washes support a large number from October to March. Total winter population around 25,000 birds.

Male Pintail

31

Shoveler
Anas clypeata ♂

Characteristics 20in (508mm). The long spatulate bill identifies this bird immediately, though its white breast, dark green head and chestnut flanks are additional distinctive features of the drake. In flight, large blue shoulder patches are obvious (less so in the female) and at close range the orange-red legs. The female is a mottled brownish bird similar to a Mallard, but the bill alone will distinguish the species. When feeding, it swims with head carried low, sieving the watery ooze for all forms of animal or vegetable matter. Occasionally it up-ends, and very infrequently dives, for food. The drake stays longer in eclipse than most other ducks and often is not in complete plumage until December.

Voice Not as vocal as some ducks. The male has a 'tuk-tuk' flight call and the female a low quacking note.

Habitat In the breeding season, open lakes and reservoirs with grassy overgrown borders, or other water areas which provide good cover for nesting. At other times it favours shallow fresh or brackish waters and very occasionally it settles on the sea.

Nest A shallow hollow, lined with grass, leaves and down, usually well hidden in lush vegetation, near to the water. The 8 to 12 eggs are greenish, laid in April to May. One brood.

Status Present throughout the year. As a breeding bird it is locally found where suitable habitat occurs, being mainly concentrated in the South East of England between the Wash and the Thames Estuary. Generally absent from Wales, the West Country and most of Scotland. It breeds sparsely in Ireland, the total population being around 1,000 pairs. In the winter, immigrants arrive from the Continent. It is most numerous in spring, when returning British breeding birds and winter visitors are present for a time; numbers may then well exceed 5,000 birds.

(left) Male ; (right) female

Pochard
Aythya ferina ♂

Characteristics 18in (457mm). Typical of the diving ducks, this bird is a familiar sight on most suitable stretches of fresh water, where it often sits for hours just dozing, or riding the waves if the weather is blowy. In good light, the rich chestnut-red colouring of the neck and head, the black breast, grey sides and back and black stern immediately identify the drake, and even in silhouette the dome-shaped head is distinctive. The female, though, is mainly a dull brown with an indistinct pale patch about the bill and chin, and also a bluish ring round the bill. It is one of the few species of duck that does not have a distinctive wing pattern, so that in flight the lack of any distinguishing marks is a feature in itself. The birds dive by gently submerging or by springing up and taking a header, depending on the depth of the water. Vegetable matter is the main life support, but some animal food is taken.

Voice Not a very vocal species, with the most frequently heard calls the alarm note 'qu-aaak' and a harsh 'currah' uttered in flight.

Habitat In the breeding season, favours lakes and large stretches of water with surrounding dense vegetation, reeds, etc. At other times, open fresh waters with or without surrounding cover, sometimes tidal estuaries.

Nest A platform of reed stems and leaves, lined with down. On the ground in dense vegetation near the water. The 8 to 10 eggs are green-grey and oval, laid late April, early May. One brood.

Status Present throughout the year, being a scarce or local breeding bird with a bias towards Eastern areas in England. Scattered breeding in Scotland, sporadic occurrences in Ireland. The total British and Irish breeding population is probably not over 500 pairs, but the winter population must be over 50,000 birds, being supplemented by visitors from E Europe and Russia.

(above) Female; (below) male

33

Tufted Duck
Aythya fuligula ♀

Characteristics 17in (432mm). Undoubtedly our best known diving duck, the drake with its distinctive black and white plumage, rounded head, crest and golden-yellow eye is easily identified. The female's plumage pattern is similar, except the black areas are dark brown and the flanks are a paler brown, not white, making it harder to identify, especially at a distance when mixed in with other species of duck. It dives with a distinct jump, submerging for around 15 seconds to feed on a wide variety of animal life and plant matter. Flight is rapid, and a distinctive white wing bar is then visible. Some females have varying amounts of white around the base of the bill though never as much as the female Scaup *(Aythya marila)*, and are often whitish under the tail.

Voice The usual note is a growling 'kurr-kurr' uttered in flight. Courting drakes have a musical whistling.

Habitat Open fresh water, with reeds or other cover. Quiet stretches of rivers and particularly in recent years sand and gravel pits. Occasionally sheltered coastal waters are visited, also urban park lakes where Tufted Duck can become quite tame. Very rare on the sea.

Nest A depression in the ground, lined with grass, rushes, reeds and down, usually well hidden in vegetation close to the water. Often on small islands, where a number may nest in close proximity. The 8 to 11 eggs are greenish-grey, laid in May and June. One brood.

Status Present throughout the year and breeding widely in Britain (except SW), though scarce or absent from NW Scotland, Wales. In Ireland not found in the major part of the SE. Since the first nesting record in Yorkshire in 1849, this has become one of our most successful breeding wildfowl, with a total British and Irish population currently around 6,000 pairs. In winter immigrant birds swell the total to an estimated 50,000 birds.

Similar or Allied Species The Scaup *(Aythya marila)* lacks the Tufted Duck's crest and its back is grey. The female resembles the female Tufted, but has an extensive whitish area around the base of the bill. A marine species (unusual inland), occurring in large numbers on certain estuaries in winter; particularly abundant on the Firth of Forth.

(above, left) Female and (right) male Scaup;
(below, left) female and (right) male Tufted Duck

Eider

Somateria mollisima ♀

Characteristics 23in (584mm). The male is the only duck with a black belly and white back, which, with its large size, bulky appearance and sloping forehead, make it unmistakable. However the brown female, mottled and barred with black, has little beyond size and shape that can be called distinctive. Highly sociable at all times, the Eider congregates at its coastal breeding colonies during the summer, and in winter large groups are to be found scattered along coasts and inshore waters. It feeds mainly at low tide, diving for crustaceans and molluscs, mussels being especially favoured and usually eaten under water. Flight is steady and direct, often only a few feet above the waves, usually in single file.

Voice Extremely vocal, especially during courtship when the male makes various 'coo-ing' calls, particularly a loud 'coo-roo-uh'. The female has a grating 'corr'.

Habitat It prefers steep, rocky, spray-swept coasts, being strongly maritime, only exceptionally going inland.

Nest On the ground, usually in the shelter of a rock or in deep vegetation but frequently quite exposed, invariably near the shore. Nesting material includes grass, heather or seaweed and the birds' own down. (Eiders are still farmed for their down in Iceland and parts of Scandinavia).

Status A resident. Has been expanding and steadily increasing its range since the middle of the nineteenth century. It breeds extensively in the Orkneys, Shetlands and Hebrides, also on the E Scottish coast southwards to the Farne Islands. Also nests along parts of N Irish coast. Total British and Irish breeding population around 20,000 pairs. Winter population probably at least double this figure.

Male Eider and (foreground) male Eider assuming adult plumage

Goldeneye
Bucephala clangula ♂

Characteristics 18in (457mm). The adult drake is a boldy patterned black and white bird with a large white spot at the base of the bill below and in front of the eye. Though not so striking, the female is no less distinctive, having a dark brown head with a white collar. Immature birds are similar to the female but lack the white collar. At all ages, both sexes have a peaked crown, giving the head a distinctive triangular-shaped appearance accentuated by the short bill. It rises more rapidly from the water than other diving ducks and in flight the wings make a characteristic whistling note. The prominent white patches on the wing also help identification. Extremely active, the Goldeneye dives constantly, disappearing under the water for up to a minute as its searches for molluscs or crustaceans, on which it lives almost exclusively, though some insects are taken. In the early part of the year, groups of males display to one another, throwing the head back and raising the breast at the same time, uttering a strange grating note similar to the winding-up of a watch.

Voice Usually silent except when displaying.

Habitat In the breeding season, lakes with surrounding forest (with hollow trees). In the winter, frequents coastal waters and also inland lakes and reservoirs.

Nest In a hole in a tree, lined with a few wood chips and some down; it will also readily use nest boxes. The 6 to 15 eggs are bluish-green, laid mid-April onwards. One brood.

Status Mainly a winter visitor, with large flocks to be found on estuaries and around some coasts. Small numbers occur at favoured inland waters. The winter population is between 10,000 and 15,000 birds. It has nested every year since 1970, when the first fully authenticated record was obtained in Inverness-shire, Scotland. It is now firmly established as a breeding bird in that area, partly due to extensive provision of nest boxes, though the numbers are small. A Schedule I bird.

Similar or Allied Species Long-tailed Duck (*Clangula hyemalis*) is a common sea duck but infrequent close inshore and rare inland. A small diving duck, it occurs in a variety of plumages.

Male Goldeneye (foreground) displays to the female

Red-breasted Merganser

Mergus serrator ♂

Characteristics 23in (584mm). Though more maritime than the similar Goosander, both may occur together on either salt or fresh water, when the Merganser can be distinguished by its slightly smaller size and wispy double crest. The drake has a greenish-black head, separated from the chestnut breast by a white collar, the flanks vermiculated with grey, the bill red. The female is much less distinct, being brownish-grey with a rufous brown head which shades gradually at the neck and is not as clear-cut as in the Goosander. There is also a dingy white throat patch, again much less defined than in the Goosander. It swims low in the water, diving frequently for fish, often small groups feeding together. Flight is low and fast over the sea, when the white patches on the wing crossed by two black bands can be seen. A black band also crosses the female's white speculum, which is absent in the Goosander.

Voice Usually silent but it has a variety of rough calls during courtship. The female has a loud harsh 'ar-r-r' like the Goosander.

Habitat In the breeding season, lakes and broad rivers, lochs with adjacent woodland. At other times coastal areas, preferring sheltered bays and estuaries.

Nest A shallow depression lined with grass, leaves and down, sited in a hollow among tree roots, in a crevice, or under thick vegetation, never far from water. The eggs, 8 to 10, are stone or buff colour, laid in late May. One brood.

Status Present throughout the year. As a breeding bird it is concentrated in Scotland, mainly in western areas; it also breeds in the Orkneys and Shetlands. In recent years it has expanded its range into NE England, Anglesey and N Wales. It has also increased its range in Ireland, mainly in the W. Total breeding population is probably over 2,000 pairs. In winter, migrant birds from Scandinavia and Iceland possibly increase the numbers to between 5,000 and 10,000 birds.

Similar or Allied Species The Smew (*Mergus albellus*) is a small sawbill, occasionally met in winter. The drake is mostly white, with a dark patch through the eye, while the female has a red-brown head and a white face patch and might be confused with the Ruddy Duck or even female Long-tailed Duck or Common Scoter.

Female Merganser

Goosander
Mergus merganser ♂

Characteristics 26in (660mm). Whereas the previous species leads an almost totally marine existence, the Goosander is predominantly a fresh water bird. Largest of the saw-billed ducks (having a serrated edge to the bill enabling it to catch fish more easily), it is even larger than a Mallard. Out on the water it looks long and low with the dark greenish-black head appearing quite bulbous. The red bill is long, hooked at the tip, darker and stouter than the Merganser's. The breast and under-parts are creamy white but close to they show a pinky hue. The female plumage is less contrasting, a dark brown head (with a conspicuous crest), white chin and greyish body. In flight it is more reminiscent of a diver than a duck, with the extensive area of white in the wings giving it a marked black and white appearance. It will rest and preen on the shore for long periods. When feeding, it dives for fish, staying underwater at times for over half a minute.

Voice Normally silent except when displaying, then the male utters low croaking notes. The female has a hoarse guttural 'ka-r-r'.

Habitat In the breeding season, rivers, lakes and lochs in forested areas. Outside the breeding season, large estuaries, lakes, rivers and reservoirs.

Nest Usually in the hole of a tree, generally close to the water; little material is used other than down. The 8 to 11 eggs, creamy white, are usually laid early April. One brood.

Status Present throughout the year. Since the late 1880s it has extended its breeding range in Scotland and N England, with probably up to 2,000 pairs now nesting. In the last decade, the first breeding records have been noted in Wales and Ireland. With some migrants from Scandinavia the winter population is probably around 5,000 pairs.

Female

RAH.

38

Ruddy Duck
Oxyjura jamaciensis ♂ ♂

Characteristics 13½-17in (343-432mm). With its dumpy rich chestnut body, black cap, white cheeks and bright blue bill, the drake cannot really be confused with any other duck. However it does not always show itself, keeping to the reedy margins in its breeding habitat. The duck has a blue-grey bill, a dark brown cap and nape, the buff-white cheeks crossed by a brown line from the base of the bill to the nape. Non breeding birds are similar but have a greyer bill with the red-brown areas replaced by brown. When observed for any length of time it will be noted that the Ruddy Duck often swims with the tail cocked and frequently dives, or on occasions just sinks below the surface. Food is a mixture of insect larvae and aquatic plant seeds obtained by sieving the oozy mud bottoms.

Voice Practically silent, with most sounds made mechanically during its courtship display — low belching or bumping noises made as it disturbs the water in front of its breast, producing a bubbling effect.

Habitat In the breeding season, smallish pools and lakes, sand and gravel lagoons with plenty of surrounding vegetation. In winter, it moves to larger water, reservoirs particularly, with flocks developing from September to December and dispersing in early spring.

Nest A platform of rush or reed stems with a small cup lined with a little down. The 6 to 10 eggs are creamy white, often becoming stained, laid from May onwards. One brood.

Status A North American species, there is an English population derived from escapees from Slimbridge in the 1960s. It is an established English breeding bird, mainly in the Midlands, Somerset and Avon. On one Midland reservoir a winter flock of over 300 birds is a regular feature. More widespread dispersal in hard weather. The total breeding population may be over 50 pairs.

Female

Common Scoter
Melanitta nigra ♀♂

Characteristics 19in (483mm). This seagoing duck is usually seen in large straggling flocks, swimming just too far off shore to be clearly visible. The drake, however, is totally black, its one spot of colour an orange patch on the bill, only detectable if the bird can be observed close to. The female is brownish, with a light grey cheek. The Common Scoter often flies in long formations, generally low over the waves, and then the lack of wing pattern and any other distinguishing feature is in itself indicative of the species. When swimming at ease it carries its pointed tail in an elevated position very like a Pintail. It constantly raises itself from the water and flaps its wings after its frequent dives for the molluscs of various kinds on which it mainly lives.

Voice Flocks on the sea have various whistling, piping and hooting notes, but are generally too far away to be heard!

Habitat Predominantly marine, preferring shallow inshore water. In the breeding season, lochs on hilly moorland are usually favoured, but in Ireland inland lakes with wooded islands. Small flocks of migrating birds are often noted at large inland waters, usually in early spring and late autumn and also frequently in midsummer.

Nest A hollow lined with grass and moss, lichen and down, well concealed, usually near the water.

The 6 to 8 eggs are cream to buff, laid early June. One brood.

Status One of our commonest marine ducks, to be seen in varying numbers virtually anywhere around the coast at almost any time of year, with a winter population probably over 35,000. First bred in Scotland in 1855 and Ireland in 1905. About 50 pairs now breed annually in Scotland and about 150 pairs in Ireland, mainly in the NW. A Schedule I bird.

Similar or Allied Species The Velvet Scoter (*Melanitta fusca*). Both sexes are distinguished from the Common Scoter by white wing patches often only visible when the bird flaps its wings or when flying. The female has two whitish patches on the side of the head. A winter visitor, less numerous than the Common Scoter.

(left) Male Common Scoter ; (right) Velvet Scoter

Red Kite
Milvus milvus

Characteristics 24-25in (610-635mm). A magnificent bird on the wing, and most likely to be seen in the typical gliding flight which gave it one of its old names, Glead or Gled. Superficially it resembles a buzzard when performing its effortless aerial manoeuvres, but in silhouette its angled wings and long deeply forked tail clearly differentiate it. Even when the tail is fanned and the forking less obvious, in a good light the brownish plumage, pale head, whitish patches in the wing, and chestnut-red colour of the tail feathers identify it. Also, when seen from above, pale diagonal bars across the wing are a noticeable feature. The sexes are similar. It preys on animals up to the size of a rabbit and sometimes manages to catch birds, but is undoubtedly more of a scavenger than a hunter and partial to carrion of any sort; it also eats large insects and worms. During winter particularly it is strongly gregarious and small roosts can occur, sometimes with 12 or more birds together. This number is also occasionally noted at favoured feeding areas.

Voice A quiet bird, but occasionally it gives a shrill mewing note, similar to the Buzzard's but higher-pitched and more rapidly repeated.

Habitat Wooded hillsides, open country and upland pastures.

Nest A large structure of sticks reinforced with earth and lined with rags, wool, paper and other rubbish, usually built close to the main trunk of a tree. The 2 to 3 eggs are dull white marked with reddish or purplish brown, laid in April. One brood.

Status Due to persecution by man it is a much reduced species throughout Europe and is now absent from many areas where it formerly nested. It was a common bird in England and Wales up until the end of the eighteenth century, scavenging in towns and cities. By the beginning of the twentieth century, only a dozen or so birds were left in Wales. Due to the work of the Kite Committee, set up to protect and study this remnant population, and the RSPB, the number of breeding birds has now increased to around 30 pairs. The activities of egg collectors and disturbance at the nest still threaten this most vulnerable bird. A Schedule I bird.

41

Hen Harrier
Circus cyaneus ♀

Characteristics 17-20in (432-508mm). The male is most distinctive, largely silvery-grey in colour with a white rump and black primaries. At a distance it looks so pale that it might even be confused with a gull. However, it shows typical harrier flight, as it closely and diligently quarters the ground in an easy, buoyant way, wings held in a shallow V, occasionally hovering. In this manner it pounces on its prey, mainly voles, mice, frogs, lizards, etc, but on occasions it will also chase and seize small birds. The female and immature Hen Harriers look completely different, with dark brown upper-parts and broadly streaked buffish under-parts, a long barred tail and white rump. At close quarters the face has an owl-like appearance.

Voice Usually silent except at the nest when a rapid chattering 'chik-ik-ik-ik-ik' note is uttered.

Habitat In the breeding season, moorland, bracken-covered hillsides, peat bogs and young conifer plantations. In winter, open country, salt marshes, dunes, deserted airfields, reedbeds.

Nest On the ground, amongst heather, where it creates a shallow cup lined with finer materials. In wetter areas it builds a platform of reeds or sedges. The 4 to 6 eggs are bluish-white, sometimes with spots and streaks of reddish-brown, laid in April to May. One brood.

Status Formerly widespread as a breeding bird, but because of agricultural development and persecution was virtually confined to the Orkneys, Outer Hebrides and Ireland by the beginning of this century. Due to protection and more enlightened land management it has re-established itself on the mainland of Scotland and in recent years has spread to parts of northern England and Wales. It is still increasing, with a total population of probably 600 pairs.

Similar or Allied Species Montagu's Harrier *(Circus pygargus)* is slightly smaller and slimmer with narrower, more pointed wings and noticeably more buoyant flight. The male is similar in appearance to the Hen Harrier but has narrow black bars in the centre of the wing and grey rump. The female is nearly identical with the female Hen Harrier, but juveniles have rufous under-parts. A very scarce breeding bird and occasional passage migrant. A Schedule I bird. The Marsh Harrier *(Circus aeruginosus)* is found almost exclusively in reedy areas, its behaviour similar to that of Montagu's. The male has a dark mantle and secondary wing coverts contrasting with a grey tail and secondaries. The under-parts are rich brown and the buffish head, nape and breast are streaked. The female is dark brown except for pale head and shoulders. A few pairs nest at one or two localities in East Anglia. A Schedule I bird.

Male Hen Harrier

Sparrowhawk
Accipiter nisus ♀

Characteristics 11-15in (279-381mm). When hunting this bird flies fast and low, with three or four beats of its rounded wings followed by a long glide. Moving along hedgerows, the borders of woods, woodland rides and watercourses it surprises small birds which it captures with its talons, thrusting out its long yellow legs to do so. It also shows incredible flying skill as it threads through a wood or copse to pursue any prey that escapes the first pass. It will also chase and outfly birds in the open, frequently singling out starlings. The luckless prey is always taken to a regular plucking post, usually a tree stump or small mound. The female has dark brownish upper-parts, with a white stripe above and behind the eye, and whitish under-parts finely barred with dark brown. The much smaller male has a slaty-blue-grey back and under-parts finely barred with reddish-brown. During the breeding season a pair will soar together at a considerable height over the breeding territory.

Voice Has a variety of calls in the breeding season, the usual alarm note near the nest being a rapid harsh 'kek-kek-kek-kek'.

Habitat Coniferous and mixed woodland and particularly cultivated areas with scattered woods—almost anywhere with some tree cover.

Nest A flat untidy platform of twigs, especially larch or birch. Commonly in conifer, usually close to the main trunk 20 or more feet (6m) above the ground, the old nest of Crow or Pigeon often used to form the base. The 5 to 6 eggs are bluish-white or pale green, blotched or streaked with chocolate brown, or sometimes unmarked, laid in May. One brood.

Status Present throughout the year. A very common and widespread breeding bird until the early 1960s when its population suddenly dropped and it disappeared over a wide area of England. Toxic chemicals were probably often the cause, the birds accumulating lethal doses of hydrochlorinated carbon compounds ingested by the insectivorous and seed-eating birds on which they preyed. Restrictions on the use of such chemicals are only now beginning to show results, Sparrowhawks returning to areas from which they have long been absent. Still scarce in Central and Eastern England. Total British and Irish population now possibly around 25,000 pairs. A Schedule I bird.

43

Buzzard
Buteo buteo

Characteristics 20-22in (508-559mm). The broad wings, rounded tail and short-necked appearance of this bird are evident as it soars majestically in wide spirals with little or no movement of the wings, the tips of the upward-curved primaries separated like the fingers of a hand. In some areas it is not unusual to see a dozen or more birds wheeling in the sky together. On such occasions it will be noticed that the amount of white on the under-side varies considerably, as does the pattern on the wings. Usually there is a dark patch in the carpal region, though this is never as well defined in the Rough-legged Buzzard *(Buteo lagopus)*. Sits for long periods in a tree or on top of a telegraph pole watching for prey, and in this position it is a dull-looking bird with brown upper-parts and yellow legs, lacking all the drama it has in flight. Rabbits are an important part of its diet, but it also takes small birds and earthworms, beetles, etc.

Voice A long plaintive challenging 'pee-oo', usually uttered in flight but also when perched, loud and far-carrying.

Habitat Hilly country, with wooded valleys, open moorland, secluded open regions.

Nest A bulky affair of sticks and small branches lined with other available finer materials. In moorland areas, heather is a major item. A nest in use is adorned with sprays of greenery (pine, larch, etc) and is situated in a tree or on a cliff ledge. The 2 to 3 eggs are dull white, smeared, blotched or spotted with chocolate-brown, laid in early May. One brood.

Status Mainly distributed down the western half of Britain with concentrations in W Scotland, the Lake District, Wales and SW England. A small number breed in Northern Ireland. Total population probably around 10,000 pairs.

Similar or Allied Species The Rough-legged Buzzard *(Buteo lagopus)* has longer narrower wings, a white tail with a broad dark band and conspicuous dark carpal patches. A scarce winter visitor, but some years small invasions occur. The Honey Buzzard *(Pernis apivorus)* has narrow-based broad wings, long tail and small head. Its flight silhouette is different from the Rough-legged's, and plumage is variable. It digs out bees' and wasps' nests. A summer visitor, and a small number breed in S England. A Schedule I bird.

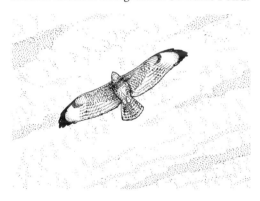

Buzzard

Golden Eagle

Aquila chrysaëtos ♀

Characteristics 30-35in (762-889mm). The majestic soaring flight recalls the Buzzard, and as at a distance the much greater size might not be apparent, confusion between the two species is possible. However, the Golden Eagle looks much more solid, less flexible, with slower, wider spiralling. At close range, size alone should be sufficient for identification, and the eagle's powerful bill gives the head a completely different appearance. The uniformly dark chocolate-brown plumage, with a yellowish tinge to the head, is typical of both adults, but young birds have white wing patches and a white tail with black band. Food varies according to availability, but Grouse, Ptarmigan and mountain hares form a major part. Other mammals and birds are certainly taken and in coastal areas, sea birds feature prominently amongst its prey. Like most eagles, it also eats carrion.

Voice Usually silent but occasionally it gives a Buzzard-like whistling note. Also has a shrill yelping cry.

Habitat Wild barren mountainous areas and less frequently in forested areas or on sea cliffs.

Nest A bulky structure of sticks, branches, heather stems and bracken, lined with grass, ferns and other fresh material. The traditional eyrie is on a cliff ledge or sometimes in a tree. A pair often use several sites in rotation. The eggs, usually 2, are dull white, flecked and spotted with red-brown and grey; often one egg is unmarked. Laid in early April. One brood.

Status Persecution finally exterminated this bird from its former English and Welsh haunts by the middle of the nineteenth century, and greatly reduced the numbers in Scotland. There has been some recovery in Scotland in recent years with greater protection, and it has recolonised some areas. Since 1969 it has also bred in England. It is still illegally shot and trapped and nests are robbed. Total population around 300 pairs. None in Ireland. A Schedule I bird.

Similar or Allied Species The White-tailed Eagle (*Haliaetus albicilla*) has a short wedge-shaped white tail but no black band. It never has white wing patches. It formerly bred in some numbers, now a rare visitor. A Schedule I bird.

Immature Golden Eagle

45

Osprey
Pandion haliaetus

Characteristics 20-23in (508-584mm). This bird's spectacular plunge-dive when securing its prey is one of the great thrills of birdwatching, and even in ordinary flight the Osprey is a truly magnificent creature. No other eagle-like bird has contrasting dark upper-parts, white under-parts and dusky breast band, and its association with water should also preclude confusion with any other species. When fishing it usually circles round 30-100ft (9-30m) above the water with alternate flaps and glides on angled wings until it sees a fish swimming near the surface; then, after hovering briefly with legs dangling, it plunges into the water, sometimes completely submerging; on reappearing it seems to have some difficulty in clearing the water, especially if the fish is large. It is not successful at every dive, but when a fish is secured it flies off with the prey held in its feet, to feed at some quiet spot. The young bird is like the adult, even to the crest, but has buff edgings to its feathers which can give it a spotted appearance.

Voice A shrill musical whistle repeated several times, dropping a pitch towards the end of the sequence. It has various other notes when alarmed or excited.

Habitat Large lakes, rivers, sea coasts.

Nest A large bulky structure of sticks, often with other materials worked in, such as heather stems, seaweed, etc, and generally lined with grass and a feather or two. The traditional site is on top of a tall conifer, usually but not always near water. The eggs, usually 3, are whitish, boldly blotched and spotted with dark chocolate or red-brown. One brood.

Status Eliminated as a breeding bird in Britain by the end of the nineteenth century due to persecution by gamekeepers and collectors. In the mid 1950s it began nesting again and after four unsuccessful years three young were raised at Loch Garten in 1959. This success was due to intensive protection by the RSPB who have guarded the site ever since. Controlled access and viewing from a specially constructed observation hide has allowed thousands of people to see these birds without disturbing them. Recolonisation has continued steadily and Ospreys are now nesting at several locations in N Scotland. Migrating birds occur at inland waters in spring and autumn. A Schedule I bird.

Kestrel

Falco tinnunculus ♀♂

Characteristics 13-14in (330-356mm). The hovering flight of this bird identifies it immediately, for no other hawk has so perfected this mode of hunting. It hangs 30ft (9m) or more above the ground on rapidly quivering wings, the tail frequently adjusted according to wind speed. The head is held down scanning the ground for any movement that indicates the presence of a vole, fieldmouse or perhaps even smaller prey such as a beetle or other insect. Having sighted its quarry it dives headlong with almost closed wings to secure the creature in its talons. It is not always successful, but usually rises from the ground clutching its victim, which it devours at some quiet spot or regular 'plucking post'. In direct flight the long tail and pointed wings are distinctive. It often spends long periods perched just surveying the scene. The male has a slate-grey head, rump and tail, the tail having a black sub-terminal band and white tip. The back is rufous, spotted with black, the under-parts buff with black streaks and spots. The bill and legs are yellow. The larger female is less colourful with rufous-brown with blackish barrings above, and paler below with dark streaks. The tail is barred.

Voice The usual cry is a shrill 'kee-kee-kee'. It is often noisy at the nest site with variations of this, but is generally silent at other times.

Habitat Woods, farmland, parks, moorland, coastal areas, derelict land, industrial sites and city centres. Frequently noted along roadside grass verges.

Nest Uses old nests of Crows or other large birds, but often nests in a hollow tree, church tower or other building, including ventilation openings and window ledges of factories or office blocks, or sometimes on the ground, particularly in the heather. The 4 to 5 eggs are whitish, heavily marked with dark red-brown, laid in mid-April. One brood.

Status Present throughout the year. Our most numerous and widespread bird of prey, breeding in all of Britain except the Shetlands and Ireland. Total population approaching 100,000 pairs.

Merlin
Falco columbarius ♀

Characteristics 10½-13in (267-330mm). This small dark-looking falcon flies low and fast on narrow pointed wings, virtually hugging the contours of the land, only allowing the briefest of glimpses before it disappears over a rise in the ground or flips over a hedge or stone wall. Small birds form the major part of its diet, and these are secured in a usually short, twisting, turning chase, when the Merlin's agility and manoeuvrability are evident. When fortunate enough to witness a chase, the observer will see that the male is slaty-blue above, with a broad black terminal band on the tail, and the rufous under-parts are heavily streaked; the long yellow legs are thrust forward at the point of seizure. If the larger female is seen, perhaps only the distinctly barred brown and cream tail will register, for the dark brown back and streaky under-parts are not so distinctive when the bird is in full flight. Lacks the rufous tinge of the female Kestrel.

Voice On the nesting ground, utters a rapid shrill grating chatter, 'kik, kik, kik-ik-ik', slightly lower-pitched in the female.

Habitat In the breeding season the Merlin is a bird of upland areas, preferring open moorland and fell country, but it also frequents sea cliffs and coastal dunes. At other times, open country, low-lying coastal areas.

Nest A scrape in thick cover of heather or bracken, often on sloping ground or near the top of a hill or gully. The eggs, 4 to 5, thickly and evenly covered with reddish-brown stipplings, laid in early May. One brood.

Status Present throughout the year. Not a common bird, but nests widely in Scotland, N England, Wales, SW England and Ireland where suitable habitat occurs. Total population probably under 1,000 pairs. A Schedule I bird.

Hobby
Falco subbuteo ♂

Characteristics 12-14in (305-356mm). Most graceful and agile of British falcons, the flying performance of this bird is not excelled by any other bird of prey, except perhaps the Peregrine. With long scythe-like wings, the Hobby is capable of capturing even such speedy fliers as Swifts. Particularly active at dusk, it often preys on Swallows and Martins, visiting their roosts in autumn. It also feeds on large flying insects such as dragonflies, which are captured with the feet and then transferred to the bill while still in flight. Not only is this species a master of the air, but it is also one of our most handsome birds of prey, having dark slaty upper-parts, broad black moustachial stripes, white neck and under-parts with conspicuous black streaks, and rusty red thighs (streaked in the female) and under-tail coverts. The female is slightly larger than the male. During the breeding season a pair might be seen performing spectacular aerobatics or indulging in long soaring flights; also it is not uncommon for the male to pass food to the female while on the wing.

Voice Quite noisy at the nest site, and also often calls when away from it. The usual note is a clear 'kew-kew-kew-kew-kew', frequently repeated.

Habitat Dry heathland and downland, open woodland and parkland, also farmland with tall hedgerow trees.

Nest Frequently in pine trees in southern areas of Britain, but commonly in deciduous trees, taking over old nests — of Carrion Crow mainly, but at times those of other species. The 2 to 4 eggs are closely speckled all over with reddish-brown, laid in late May. One brood.

Status A summer visitor, arriving late April, departing September or October. A relatively scarce bird and mainly confined to southern counties of England, with the New Forest area a particular stronghold. Total population around 100 pairs. A Schedule I bird.

Hobby in pursuit of a Swallow

49

Peregrine
Falco peregrinus ♀

Characteristics 15-19in (381-483mm). This bird, stooping at its prey, is one of the most spectacular sights in nature, and no description can quite convey its drama. Estimates of the speed achieved have been put at 100 mph (160 kmph) or more; aerodynamically it is probably capable of this, but probably rarely exceeds 65-85 mph (104-136 kmph). The great bird-of-prey expert, Leslie Brown, reckons this is its normal speed and quite sufficient to despatch its victim, which it does with its powerful hind claw. A compact, robust-looking bird with long pointed wings and medium-length tapering tail, its normal flight is swift and direct with a few rapid wing beats, alternating with a long glide. It can then look quite pigeon-like, though the dark blue-grey upper-parts, crown and side of head, with fierce black moustachial stripe, should quickly determine its identity. The pale under-parts are heavily barred, more so on the female, which is larger. In falconry terms, the female is called the falcon, the male the 'tiercel'. Like all birds of prey the Peregrine sits for long periods, often hunched on a stone, rock or cliff ledge.

Voice The main cry is a harsh, chattering 'kek-kek-kek-kek' or a rasping 'kraah-kraah-kraah'. It can be very noisy, especially at the nest site when it has young.

Habitat Wild open country, both mountain and moorland, and rocky coastal areas in particular. In the winter, coastal marshes and estuaries.

Nest A scrape, usually on a ledge or in a hole in a cliff face. Occasionally uses an old nest, of Raven or Hooded Crow. Some traditional sites are used year after year. The 3 or 4 eggs are oval-shaped, creamy-buff, generally covered by red-brown markings, usually laid mid-April. One brood.

Status Present throughout the year. Formerly more widespread; many were shot during World War II in an attempt to protect carrier pigeons. In the mid-1950s, too, it declined, due to the effects of organo-chlorine poisoning. It is making a slow recovery due to greater protection, though still harassed by egg collectors and by removal of young from the nest. Most of the breeding population is in Scotland, with some in N England, Wales and SW England. It nests sparsely in Ireland. The total British and Irish population is probably around 500-750 pairs. A Schedule I bird.

Peregrine stoops at its prey

Red Grouse

Lagopus lagopus ♂

Characteristics Male 14-15½in (356-394mm). Female 13-14in (330-356mm). Once considered to be the most British of birds, not occurring anywhere else in the world, recent thinking by taxonomists has lumped the Red Grouse with the Willow Grouse, which is found in Scandinavia eastwards across N Russia. Whether exclusive to Britain or not, the Red Grouse still features large in the British sporting calendar when 'the Glorious Twelfth' (12 August) signals the opening of the shooting season. A characteristic game bird, it is stout and short-winged, a basically ground-feeding species. The rufous-brown plumage looks very dark at a distance, and only at close quarters can the white feathered legs and red wattle over the eye be seen. When flushed it rises with whirring wings, usually calling loudly. Its rapid wing beats, followed by long glides on down-curved wings, are distinctive, and when viewed from below the striking white under-wing pattern contrasting with the dark belly is diagnostic. It feeds mainly on young heather shoots, also on buds and berries. The young chicks eat predominantly insects.

Voice The usual note when flushed is a cackling 'kowk-kok-ok-ok-ok' with variations. In the breeding season, it utters a strident 'go bak, go-bak, bak-bak-bak-bak'.

Habitat Open tree-less moorland, particularly with heather, but grassy moorland is acceptable where crowberry or bilberry occur. Also to be found on low-lying bog land where there is suitable food. In the autumn will visit stubble fields and even hawthorns.

Nest A scrape in heather or long grass, scantily lined with grass, moss or heather, feathers added during incubation. The 6 to 11 eggs are yellowish-white, blotched all over with dark chocolate-brown, laid in April to May. One brood.

Status Present throughout the year. Mainly concentrated in Scotland and N England, southwards along the Pennines to North Staffordshire where suitable habitat exists. Also found in parts of Wales with small numbers on Dartmoor and Exmoor. In Ireland it is mainly to be found in central areas and the NW. Total British and Irish population probably around half a million pairs.

Ptarmigan
Lagopus mutus ♂ S

Characteristics 13-14in (330-356mm). This grouse-like bird of the mountains is unlikely to be confused with the Red Grouse, for it always has white wings and varying amounts of white elsewhere in its plumage and in the winter is completely white, except for the white-tipped black tail and, in the male, black lores. In summer, however, the male has richly mottled blackish-brown upper-parts, breast and flanks, which in autumn become finely barred and vermiculated with grey. The female is a browner-looking bird in summer, but also has an autumn plumage change, when it looks much yellower. Both sexes have feathered feet, and have a red wattle over the eye, much smaller in the female. Juveniles look much like summer adults but have blackish primaries. Flight is similar to that of the Grouse, though it is often loath to fly and can be extremely tame and approachable; very fond of sunbathing and dusting. It feeds mainly on bilberry and crowberry, also some seed and insect matter.

Voice The usual note is a low croak, but also has a prolonged cackling call. The male utters a short crowing 'er-ook-oora' during the display flight.

Habitat The alpine zone of mountainous areas from around 2,500ft (760m). In winter it may temporarily come down lower.

Nest A scrape, scantily lined with grass or heather, usually in rather open situations but often sheltered by a stone or mound. The 5 to 9 eggs resemble those of the Red Grouse, but are smaller and usually paler, laid in late May. One brood.

Status Present throughout the year but confined to the Scottish Highlands of Aberdeenshire, Sutherland, Ross-shire, Inverness-shire, Banffshire and Perthshire. Total population probably between 10,000 and 50,000 pairs.

Winter plumage R.A.H.

52

Black Grouse
Lyrurus tetrix ♀

Characteristics Male 20-22in (508-559mm). Female 16-17in (406-432mm). There should be no problem identifying the male, which has a most distinctive combination of glossy black plumage set off by extensive white wing bars, particularly evident in flight. The white under-wing is another striking feature as the bird rises from the ground. Flight is typically grouse-like, with rapid beats of stiffly held wings followed by long glides, but this bird tends to fly higher than the Red Grouse and invariably makes a large circle before landing — providing a chance to observe its other diagnostic feature, the large lyre-shaped tail which is peculiar to this bird. The female looks quite different and is commonly known as the Grey Hen; the plumage is really a richly marked reddish-brown, but not as ruddy as the Red Grouse and without the contrasting darker wings. The female also has the distinctive white under-wing, but lacks the white wing bar and lyre-shaped tail. The male, or Blackcock as it is so often called, has a spectacular dawn courtship display, when the assembled birds dance and show off to the females by expanding and elevating white feathers under the tail with wings drooped, all of which is accompanied by a great deal of noise. The spring displays are held on traditional sites (and again in October), known as 'leks'.

Voice At lek, a series of bubbling notes which can be quite far-reaching. Other extraordinary crowing and hissing noises are also given.

Habitat Moorland-type country with heather, but additionally some trees and scrub or conifer plantation, open pine and birch woodland.

Nest A scrape on the ground in thick vegetation, with little or no lining. The eggs, 6 to 10, are yellowish-white, sparsely marked with yellow or red-brown, laid in May. One brood.

Status Present throughout the year. Formerly more widespread but now restricted to suitable areas of Scotland, where most are to be found, and to N England, the Peak district and N Staffordshire moors. Also present in parts of Wales, with a few on Exmoor and Dartmoor. None in Ireland. Total population probably around 25,000 pairs.

Male

53

Capercaillie

Tetrao urogallus

Characteristics Male 33-35in (838-889mm). Female 23-25in (584-635mm). When flushed this giant-sized bird makes a tremendous noise as its great bulk crashes its way through undergrowth, but once clear of cover it can be seen to have the regular game-bird-type flight — a succession of quick wing beats followed by prolonged glides on down-curved wings. The head is held well forward, so that quite often the male's ragged throat feathers are noticeable. Close to, the dark-looking male appears quite colourful, having a slaty-grey body, dark brown wing coverts, black head and sides of throat, and dark glossy-green breast; a front-on view shows two conspicuous white patches at the carpal joint. The tail is black with white markings, the bill is white, and above the eye is an area of bright red skin. When displaying, the body swells, the throat is distended and the tail is fanned turkey-like, the bird leaping into the air with much flapping of wings. The female is quite different, with a striking rufous tail, deep orange breast and white patches on the under-wing which can be readily seen in flight, even at long range. Though normally to be found on the ground, the Capercaillie perches freely on trees to roost and feed on conifer shoots. Buds, berries, fruits and some insects are also eaten.

Voice When displaying, makes a succession of 'clopping' noises, accelerating, to end with a loud pop and grating sound.

Habitat Coniferous woodland with a fair amount of undergrowth. In winter it can be found in other types of low-lying woodland and on occasion amongst heather. Also visits stubble fields.

Nest A scrape among ground vegetation on forest floor, usually between exposed tree-roots. Sometimes in open heather on moor. Some lining is added during egg laying. The 5 to 8 eggs are pale yellow, sparsely marked with spots and blotches of yellowish-brown, laid late April. One brood.

Status Became extinct in Britain in the middle of the eighteenth century, was reintroduced in the first half of the nineteenth, and is now established in NW Scotland, where over 10,000 pairs are probably present. Reintroduction into Ireland has so far been unsuccessful. An attempt to establish the bird in N Lancashire has met some success.

Female

Red-legged Partridge
Alectoris rufa   ♀

Characteristics 13½in (343mm). Sometimes called the 'French Partridge' or Frenchman, this and the Grey Partridge are very similar, though the heavily barred chestnut, black and white flanks, the white face surrounded by a black and white gorget, the distinctive white eye-stripe, red bill and legs, should leave no doubt about its identity. Restless and nervous, its movements on the ground are quicker than those of the Grey Partridge, but if disturbed it is less inclined to take flight, running rapidly over the furrows. In autumn it gathers in groups, called coveys, which tend to scatter when flushed. In flight it has a reddish tail, as the Grey Partridge, but the plain olive upper-parts should help to distinguish it. It feeds mainly on vegetable matter, but also eats insects, worms and slugs. The sexes are similar, though the juvenile has none of the adults' colourful plumage and is not unlike a young Grey Partridge but rather more spotted than streaked.

Voice A distinctive 'chucka-chucka-chucka' and when flushed a harsh 'kuk-kuk' note.

Habitat Agricultural country with a preference for light, dry, sandier soils and more open downland-type country. Not infrequent on coastal dunes and shingle.

Nest A scrape on the ground, scantily lined with grass and leaves, usually well concealed in thick cover, often in a hedge base. The 10 to 16 eggs are pale yellow-brown, spotted dull red and ashy, laid in April to May. The bird regularly lays two clutches in separate nests, one incubated by the male.

Status Present throughout the year. Originally introduced into England about 1673, but unsuccessfully. A century later was reintroduced in Suffolk and subsequently other areas. Now well established from Yorkshire southwards through central England to the Welsh border and East Anglia. Sparse in parts of SE England. Does not breed in the West Country. Has bred in a few scattered localities of E Scotland. None in Ireland. The total British population is estimated at between 100,000 and 200,000 pairs.

Female

Grey Partridge
Perdix perdix ♀ ♂

Characteristics 12in (305mm). Formerly known as the Common Partridge, this familiar game bird is often seen in groups or 'coveys' which stay together from autumn through to the following spring. This species lacks the distinctive white face and barring on the flanks of the Red-legged Partridge (the Frenchman), but when seen at close range is equally handsome, with pale orange-chestnut face, grey neck and breast, and a conspicuous dark chestnut horseshoe mark on the lower breast. Juveniles lack the orange-chestnut colouring, having streaked brown under-parts and neck, not unlike a young Pheasant but with a shorter tail and, of course, the bird is much smaller. If disturbed the Grey Partridge will run from danger, but it more readily takes flight than the Red-legged species, rising with a whirr of wings and flying swiftly and strongly, skimming the furrows and hedgerows, usually settling little more than a field away. Food is mainly vegetable matter, also seed, grain and some insects. The young Partridge is dependent on caterpillars during its early development and is susceptible to cold late springs.

Voice A grating 'kirr-ic, kirr-ic' repeated rapidly when excited; 'kit-it-it' when flushed.

Habitat Agricultural country, particularly where rough cover abounds, but also low moorland, heaths, marshes, dunes and not infrequently found on marginal land and allotments close to habitations.

Nest A scrape, lined with dry grass and dead leaves, usually in a hedge bottom, under a bush, in deep grass or growing crops. The 9 to 20 eggs are uniformly olive-brown and pointed, laid April to May. One brood.

Status Present throughout the year. Generally distributed in Britain, but absent from NW Scotland, Orkneys and Shetlands, and parts of Central and coastal Wales. Thinly distributed in Ireland. Has declined in recent years, particularly in S England, but present population estimated at around 50,000 pairs.

Similar or Allied Species The Quail *(Coturnix coturnix)* is much like a small Partridge, especially in flight, but has a distinctive liquid call, 'wet-my-lips'. It is a scarce summer visitor, more widely noted in some years.

Female Grey Partridge and young

56

Pheasant

Phasanius colchicus ♂

Characteristics Male 30-35in (762-889mm). Female 21-25in (533-635mm). A cock bird strutting along the furrows of a ploughed field or picking up acorns on the edge of a wood is a familiar country sight. Pheasants can also be frequently observed feeding on the grass verges of country lanes, unconcernedly risking life and limb to cross the path of an oncoming vehicle. At such times the burnished copper plumage with dark crescent markings on the breast and flanks, the dark green head, scarlet wattles and long pointed tail are more than evident. The hen is soberly attired in mottled buff and black, tail much shorter, but still lengthy. In woodland the Pheasant rockets away from under the feet in a whirr of wings, having lain invisible in the leaf litter of the forest floor. Though a terrestrial bird, obtaining food from the ground, it roosts in trees at night. Its diet includes a great deal of vegetable matter, also insects, earthworms, etc.

Voice The male has a crowing, far-reaching and distinctive 'korrk-kok', the female utters a shrill whistle when frightened or flushed.

Habitat Wooded agricultural land, parkland, open country with scattered tree plantations. At times it also haunts reed beds and damp rushy fields.

Nest A scrape on the ground, lined with grass and leaves, frequently in a hedge bottom or under brambles or bracken in woods. The 8 to 15 eggs are uniformly olive-brown, laid April to May. One brood.

Status Present throughout the year. Probably brought to Britain by the Normans in the eleventh century. Other introductions were made in the eighteenth century. Artificial rearing in considerable numbers tends to give unnatural distribution, though it survives quite well away from managed areas. It is found wherever suitable habitat occurs, being absent from some parts of Wales, NW Scotland, the Hebrides and Shetlands. Total British and Irish population may well be about half a million pairs.

Similar or Allied Species The Pheasant shows considerable variation due to the interbreeding of the two races, *Phasianus c. colchicus* from the Caucasus and *Phasianus c. torquatus* from China. Some birds can be quite dark and other males have a white ring around the neck. Two other species of Pheasant introduced are now breeding freely in the wild in some areas, and have been added to the list of British birds: the Golden Pheasant (*Chrysolophus pictus*) and Lady Amherst's Pheasant (*Chrysolophus Amherstiae*).

Female Pheasant

Water Rail
Rallus aquaticus ♂

Characteristics 11in (279mm). This bird has secretive and retiring habits, rarely providing the watcher with protracted views; usually no more than a fleeting glimpse is obtained as it races for cover when disturbed or alarmed. On such occasions it gives the impression of being a very dark bird, a lot like a slim Moorhen on the run, but with a long red slightly curved bill. When it can be seen well, perhaps feeding at the edge of a reed-fringed pond or in a ditch, its dark appearance is seen as made up of olive-brown upper-parts streaked with black, a grey head and neck and barred black and white flanks. The legs, with long toes, are brownish. The tail, with its whitish under-side, is frequently jerked, again as in Moorhen. It often swims, and does so in preference to flying across a stretch of water. When it does take to the air the flight is weak, and with its legs dangling it drops quickly into cover with a sideways swoop. Food is varied, including aquatic creatures as well as vegetable matter.

Voice A mixture of grunts, squeals and groans, reminiscent of squealing pigs. Also has a sharp 'kik, kik, kik' note. Can be very vociferous at night.

Habitat Dense aquatic vegetation, reed beds, lake margins, overgrown canals and any swampy or marshy areas with plenty of cover.

Nest Made of dead reeds and sedges, very like a small Moorhen's nest but usually well hidden in reeds or grass. The 6 to 11 eggs are creamy white, red and blue speckling often concentrated at the large end; laid from early April. Often two broods.

Status Present throughout the year. Widespread, breeding where suitable habitat exists, but not in great numbers. Total breeding population of Britain and Ireland probably around 2,000 to 3,000 pairs. Considerable influx of migrant birds around September, October.

Similar or Allied Species The Corncrake *(Crex crex)*, sometimes called the Land Rail, and a summer visitor. It proclaims its presence with its rasping, disyllabic call. Much larger than other rails, it has a buffer appearance and in flight shows conspicuous chestnut wing patches. The bill is short. It skulks in long grass in lush meadows and other vegetation. It formerly bred quite widely, now only scattered breeding occurrences in England and Wales, but can still be found regularly in the Hebrides and Orkneys, also still quite common in Ireland except extreme SW. A Schedule I bird.

Corncrake

Moorhen
Gallinula chloropus

Characteristics 13in (330mm). This waterside-haunting bird is likely to be confused only with the Coot, but whereas the latter is more often seen on the water, the Moorhen or Merehen is found along its edge, even in trees. The long green legs and feet (with a red garter above the joint) are ideal for walking over floating vegetation or across a muddy stretch of shore. The dark highly glossed plumage is really slate-coloured about the head and breast, the back being dark olive-brown. There is a distinctive white line on the flanks and the conspicuous white under-tail coverts are divided by a black line down the centre. When nervous or excited the tail is flirted in a most characteristic manner. Another colourful feature is the red frontal shield on the forehead and the red bill with yellow tip. On the water it swims buoyantly, jerking its head. When frightened it half-runs, half-flies across the water, rising with apparent difficulty, legs trailing. When surprised it will dive to escape danger, remaining submerged under the lea of the river bank or floating vegetation, with only its beak above the water. Food comprises vegetable matter, seeds, fruit, insects, tadpoles, small fish, etc. It frequently grazes on grassland or crops adjacent to the water. The sexes are similar.

Voice A loud 'squarruck', also a quick 'kittick' note with variants. Sometimes heard over suburbs at night.

Habitat Even the smallest pond is suitable for this species, also slow streams, water meadows, marshes, medium-sized lakes, reservoirs and ornamental urban waters.

Nest A well-constructed platform of reeds or other water plants, lined with finer materials. Typically in shallow water among aquatic plants or supported by a fallen branch or in a grass tussock, etc, sometimes in discarded debris such as old prams, or bicycle wheels in water. Also it frequently uses old nests of Magpie or Wood Pigeon in tall hedgerows. The 5 to 11 eggs are buff-coloured with dark red-brown blotches, laid March onwards. Two or three broods.

Status Present throughout the year, a common breeding bird in Britain and Ireland except where habitat unsuitable such as Scottish Highlands, Central Wales and parts of Dartmoor, Exmoor and extreme western Ireland. Total breeding population estimated at 300,000 pairs.

When swimming with ducks it can be distinguished by the rounded back and small head. It constantly dives for food, mainly weed, which it brings to the surface; it can remain submerged for at least half a minute. The flight is laboured and avoided if possible, but when airborne narrow white edges to the secondaries give a pale-grey appearance to the wings. The juvenile bird with its dusky grey back and white throat and neck might be confused with the Great Crested Grebe. More gregarious than the Moorhen, it forms large flocks on suitable waters during winter. The sexes are similar.

Voice Usual call is a loud 'kowk' or double 'ke-kowk', and it has various other disyllabic notes.

Habitat During breeding season, prefers large open stretches of water with marginal cover of reeds or other waterside vegetation. Outside the breeding season it frequents reservoirs, often those with concrete sides devoid of cover; also lakes and sand and gravel pits. In hard weather it will resort to the sea, remaining close to the shore, and to tidal estuaries.

Nest Quite a large structure of aquatic vegetation, with deepish cup. Usually built in water, but not floating like the Grebe's. The 4 to 8 eggs (frequently more) are stone-coloured with speckles or spots of dark brown, laid April onwards. Two, sometimes three, broods.

Status Present throughout the year. Widely distributed and locally common, it is however very scarce in NW Scotland and absent from parts of W Wales and SW England. Also sparse in parts of Ireland. Total breeding population in Britain and Ireland around 100,000 pairs.

R.A.H.

Coot
Fulica atra

Characteristics 15in (381mm). Out on the water this bird appears totally black, while at closer range the white frontal shield and bill are diagnostic and the plumage is seen to be jet-black on head and neck, but slaty on the back. An aggressive species, it frequently chases others of its kind, scuttering across the water on long greenish legs which have curiously lobed feet.

Oystercatcher
Haematopus ostralegus

Characteristics 17in (432mm). With its black and white plumage, pink legs, long orange-red bill and blood-red eye, the distinctive 'sea-pie' can be seen at any time, scattered over mudflats and along sandy shores probing for molluscs (which form the major part of its diet), crustacea and worms. Whether it ever opens oysters is doubtful, but it is certainly adept at forcing back the valves of mussels and smaller bivalves. It will also knock an unsuspecting limpet from a rock with ease. It flights in long lines, low over the sea, between feeding and roosting. It is noisy and excitable and from February through to July groups of birds frequently perform spectacular piping displays. In winter plumage it has a white half-collar on the throat.

Voice A shrill 'klee-eep, klee-eep'. The song goes into a long kleepering trill, a development of the above call. Also a short sharp 'pic-pic-pic'.

Habitat Basically a coastal species, it is found on sandy or rocky shores alike. It also occurs along rivers and around inland lochs, on the margins of reservoirs or gravel pits and even on pasture or arable fields and moorland.

Nest A large scrape, usually on shingle or sand, often unlined, but sometimes nearby debris, shell, bits of seaweed or pebbles are used. The 2 to 4 eggs are spotted, blotched and streaked dark brown or black, usually laid in May. One brood.

Status Present throughout the year. There has been a marked increase in numbers since the turn of the century, with further inland areas colonised in recent years, particularly in Scotland. Breeds round most of Britain's coastline where suitable habitat occurs, though sparse along the NE and S coasts of England. Also nests round most of Irish coastline except the south. Total breeding population probably around 30,000 pairs. In winter common on estuaries and mudflats, often in flocks of several thousand. Winter population about 200,000 birds.

Avocet
Recurvirostra avosetta

Characteristics 17in (432mm). One of our most delightful wading birds. The contrasting black and white plumage, long lead-blue legs and distinctive slender upcurved bill are unmistakable. When seen feeding, the side-to-side sweeping action is also distinctive as it sieves the watery ooze for molluscs, crustacea and worms. In deeper water, it will dip its head below the surface and it swims readily if it wades out of its depth. It will even up-end like a duck. It is probably even more attractive when seen flying, appearing mainly white if viewed from below, the black wing-tips looking less pointed than those of most other wading birds. The upper-parts with narrow black chevrons are most diagnostic, even if one fails to notice the upcurved bill or trailing legs. A very aggressive species in defence of its territory, it will run with lowered head and spread wings to drive off any offenders. Young birds have the same plumage pattern as the adult with blacks browner and white parts suffused brownish. The sexes are similar.

Voice A melodious fluty 'kluit', used as an ordinary call and as an alarm note.

Habitat In breeding season, coasts with extensive mudflats, brackish lagoons or salt marshes. In winter it frequents muddy coastal areas and estuaries.

Nest A scrape on dried mud, sometimes lined or rimmed with dried stalks. Colonial, with many nesting closely together where the site is suitable. The 3 to 4 eggs are pale buff, spotted irregularly with black and underlying ashy marks, laid early May. One brood.

Status A summer visitor, some stay through the winter. It formerly nested regularly along the east coast from the Humber to Sussex but declined during the eighteenth and nineteenth centuries, the last breeding record in Kent being in 1842. Recolonisation of the English coast began in the early 1940s at Havergate and Minsmere in Suffolk, which have remained centres of population due to work of the RSPB. At Havergate over 100 pairs have nested in good years. It leaves breeding areas in autumn, returning March to April. Around 200 winter on estuaries in SW England. A Schedule I bird.

Similar or Allied Species The Black-winged Stilt *(Hamantopus hamantopus)* has enormously long pink legs, straight black bill and contrasting black and white plumage, so is not to be mistaken when it occurs; now infrequent, though this vagrant from S Europe nested at a Nottingham sewage farm in 1954. A Schedule I bird.

Avocet

Stone Curlew
Burhinus oedicnemus

Characteristics 16in (406mm) Particularly active at dusk, it can be heard calling with its plaintive wailing note well into the night during the breeding season. Not only do its crepuscular habits limit the likelihood of its being observed during the day, but its streaked sandy-brown plumage makes it difficult to see on the stony, sandy soil it favours. If it is seen, however, its appearance is unmistakable, similar to that of a large plover with pale yellow legs and large yellow eyes. If disturbed it acts in a stealthy manner, taking short pattering steps with head lowered and neck retracted: if surprised it freezes in a flattened position, head and neck extended. Flight reveals a most conspicuous wing pattern of two bold whitish bars. It feeds principally at night, taking a variety of food, mainly snails, slugs, worms and insects. A sociable species, it occurs in small parties or groups, becoming more gregarious in the autumn.

Voice A plaintive 'coo-ee', like a shrill curlew call. A variety of wild calls on the breeding grounds.

Habitat In the breeding season, dry, stony, open ground, chalk downlands, sandy heaths and shingles, but increasingly found in cultivated fields and woodland firebreaks, as preferred habitat disappears. It may visit marshes, sea-shores and estuaries in winter or on passage.

Nest Sometimes quite a deep scrape, at other times virtually no scrape at all, but invariably lined with small stones or rabbit droppings. Usually on bare open ground or ploughed fields. Two eggs, rounded, pale buff or stone, irregularly spotted, streaked and blotched with dark brown, laid late April. Sometimes two broods.

Status A few may winter in S England, but mainly a summer visitor, the majority arriving March to April, staying until October or November. It has decreased considerably since the 1950s as a breeding bird, due to habitat loss. It is mostly found in the Brecklands of East Anglia and the downlands of Wiltshire. Probably no more than 500 pairs in any year. A Schedule I bird.

Little Ringed Plover
Charadrius dubius

Characteristics 6in (152mm). A fresh water version of the more common Ringed Plover, this species is rarely found on the coast. Its presence in the breeding season is quickly revealed by its noisy demonstrative behaviour, flying backwards and forwards over its territory, calling excitedly. On the ground it looks smaller and slimmer than the Ringed Plover, a most noticeable difference when the two are seen side by side. However, the best means of identification is the absence of any wing bar and the distinct note. At close quarters the flesh-coloured legs and lemon-yellow orbital ring are further distinguishing features. When feeding it takes a step forward and picks up some insect, worm or other invertebrate in a similar way to other plovers. It also uses foot patterning to bring food to the surface.

Voice An urgent shrill piping call 'pew'. On breeding grounds a trilling song, like that of the Ringed Plover, accompanied by a similar butterfly display flight. Most frequently heard March to July.

Habitat Gravel pits, industrial spoil tips, waste ground, reservoir margins, shingle beds of rivers.

Nest A scrape on bare ground, usually lined with small stones, rarely near vegetation but sometimes the eggs are laid on bare dried-out mud and hidden by subsequent growth. The 4 eggs, more oval than those of the Ringed Plover, are greyish-buff, finely speckled all over with small brown spots. Usually laid April to May. Sometimes two broods.

Status Summer visitor. Unknown as a breeding bird in Britain before 1938 and then rarely recorded as a migrant. In that year a pair nested in Hertfordshire. In 1949 two pairs bred at the same site and another in Middlesex. Since then has increased and spread northwards to Northumberland and eastwards to Norfolk and Suffolk. It does not breed in Wales, SW England or Ireland. Probably around 500 pairs now nest annually in Britain. A Schedule I bird.

Similar or Allied Species The Kentish Plover (*Charadrius alexandrinus*), has a dark patch either side of white breast, black bill and legs (immature Ringed and Little Ringed Plover also have an incomplete black breast band). It formerly nested in small numbers on the south coast, and is now a scarce migrant.

Kentish Plover and (foreground) Little Ringed Plover

Ringed Plover
Charadrius hiaticula

Characteristics 7½in (190mm). A small, rotund, lively shore bird, its feeding actions are typical of the plover family, running quickly for a few steps then stopping to pick up a mollusc, worm or insect. It does not normally occur in large numbers as do some other tideline feeders such as Dunlin, and it tends to be more scattered across the sandflats, the birds maintaining only loose contact with each other. However, in flight the Ringed Plover bunches into compact groups, manoeuvring in the same precise way as Dunlin or Knot. The normal direct flight is rapid and generally low down, showing a conspicuous white wing bar which precludes confusion with the Little Ringed Plover. Singled out for individual attention it will be seen that the Ringed Plover is somewhat larger than the Dunlin, with which it freely consorts, and has a prominent black collar, broad in front and narrow behind (incomplete in juvenile), a brown back and crown, orange-yellow legs (flesh-coloured in the juveniles) and an orange bill with black tip.

Voice Usual note is a liquid 'pee-u'. Also has a piping 'kluup' call. The song is a long trilling 'tooli-tooli-tooli' heard regularly from March until July, delivered in nuptial flight, when the bird flies round with slow beats of fully expanded wings in butterfly fashion.

Habitat During breeding season, sandy and shingly seashores. Also nests on fallow land, dried mud of drained marshes near the coast, sandy heathland well away from the sea, inland rivers, lakes, etc. Outside the breeding season, it winters on muddy and sandy estuaries. Frequent at inland waters on passage.

Nest A scrape on sand and shingle or turf, sometimes lined with small stones, bits of shell or rabbit droppings. Usually in an open situation, but occasionally in shelter of plants or marram. The 3 to 4 eggs are pear-shaped, buff-coloured, blackish-brown speckles or blotches often concentrated at the large end, laid end of April to May. Sometimes two broods.

Status Present all the year round. A common breeding bird, nesting in suitable areas around coasts with a stronghold in the Outer Hebrides and high-density breeding in the Orkneys, Shetlands and Norfolk. Total breeding British and Irish population over 6,000 pairs. The winter population of major estuaries is supplemented by Continental visitors and is probably around 25,000 birds.

Dotterel
Eudromias morinellus ♂

Characteristics 8½in (216mm). Individual birds can be extraordinarily tame, hence the name, but others can be quite wild, readily taking flight. In the air similarity with Golden Plover may be detected, but it looks more compact with a shorter tail. When seen from below, the white throat, pectoral band and white under-tail contrast markedly with the black under-belly, providing more obvious differences. On the ground, the general behaviour is much that of other plovers, with a short quick run, a pause, then picking up food, which is mainly insects, though also some vegetable matter. Even at a distance the very broad white eye-stripes which join in a distinct V on the nape are a most apparent feature, though in young birds and adults in autumn and winter these are duller, and of course the more clear-cut summer plumage is lacking. The legs are dull yellow. On its breeding grounds the male incubates the eggs while females gather together in small bands. On migration Dotterel are occasionally to be seen in small parties called 'trips', though to see a dozen or more together is exceptional nowadays.

Voice A soft repetitive 'twit-e-wee-wit-e-wee' developing into a trill when displaying.

Habitat In breeding season, wild and desolate mountain country. During migration, it occurs on hilltops, grassy lowlands and such places as airfields, golf courses, etc.

Nest A scrape, sometimes lined with lichen or moss, usually in a patch of vegetation, often on a slight rise. The eggs, usually 3, are oval, light to greenish buff, heavily blotched with dark brown, laid May to June. One brood.

Status A summer visitor. It formerly bred in N England and S Scotland, but breeding now is mainly confined to the Cairngorms and Grampians, probably no more than 100 breeding pairs in any season. A Schedule I bird.

Golden Plover
Pluvialis apricarius

Characteristics 11in (279mm). In summer plumage a most beautiful bird, with black belly and golden spangled upper-parts. In the winter, it loses the black on the under-parts and some of its summer lustre. It feeds in the usual plover manner, often associating with Lapwings. When a flock of Lapwings rises from a field, look for other birds with long, narrow, fast-beating wings which quickly separate themselves, flying higher and faster, calling with a different note: these are bound to be Golden Plover. On settling, it glides before landing, holding up its wings for a moment before folding them. It also has the habit of wing-stretching, and then the white under-side can indicate the bird's position, often difficult to determine when it is standing on the dark background of a ploughed field. Food includes insects, spiders, worms, vegetable matter, etc. When on shore, which is infrequent, it takes molluscs and small marine creatures.

Voice A musical liquid 'tlui' note. In breeding area, song is a rippling trill uttered in the air and on the ground, most frequently given in March to June.

Habitat In the breeding season, upland moors. In winter, grass fields, arable land, lowland hills, often returning to traditional feeding areas each year.

Nest A scrape, usually sparsely lined with heather, twigs and lichen, sometimes hidden in grass. The 3 to 4 eggs are more oval than the Lapwing's, usually creamy-buff, with bold blotches and spots of dark red-brown frequently zoned towards the large end, laid in April to May. One brood.

Status Present throughout the year. Breeds extensively in the Shetlands, Orkneys, Hebrides, Scotland, N England and southwards mainly along the Pennines to N Staffordshire moors. Some breed in Central Wales and parts of W Ireland. A small colony recently established on Dartmoor. Total British and Irish population around 30,000 pairs. Also a passage migrant and winter visitor, with perhaps as many as 200,000 present between November and February.

Winter plumage

Grey Plover
Pluvialis squatarola   W

Characteristics 11in (279mm). Closely resembles the Golden Plover but is a somewhat larger, stouter bird with silver-grey spangling instead of gold on the upper-parts. In summer plumage it has a wholly black face, lower breast and under-belly, bordered by white, a striking combination which is most likely to be seen on passage birds in late spring and early autumn. As the bird moults, varying amounts of black on the under-parts often show as a mass of black and white spots, giving it an odd appearance. In winter dress the Grey Plover is a very grey bird (juveniles have a yellowish tinge to the upper-parts), and at a distance may prove difficult to identify. However, the distinctive plover appearance and feeding manner are diagnostic. It also has a dejected, hunched look, and frequently stands on one leg, as do most waders. In flight it shows a conspicuous black armpit (axillaries) on adults and immatures alike (a feature that no other species has). There is also a prominent wing bar and a noticeably white rump and tail. Generally shy and wary, it is usually to be seen in small groups rather than in huge flocks. It feeds on molluscs, worms, crustacea, etc.

Voice A mournful trisyllabic 'tlee-oo-ee'.

Habitat Mudflats and estuaries.

Status Mainly a winter visitor and passage migrant, some birds arriving as early as July and leaving about March, with a number lingering on into June. A few stay throughout the summer, occasionally noted inland on passage around reservoir margins, sand and gravel workings and similar watery situations. Total winter population probably around 10,000 birds, possibly more.

Grey Plover, winter and (foreground) summer plumage

Lapwing
Vanellus vanellus

Characteristics 12in (305mm). The tumbling erratic display flight of the Lapwing (or Peewit) in early spring, accompanied by its distinctive call cannot be overlooked, and identification of this most familiar of wading birds is no problem. In normal direct flight it is equally distinctive, and even at considerable range the slow beats of the broad, rounded wings give a distinctive flickering black-and-white appearance as the birds lazily trail across the sky in straggling lines. At rest the long crest is very apparent while close observation will reveal the dark upper-parts are in fact metallic green and the under-tail coverts a rufous buff (particularly obvious when the bird comes in to land), the legs reddish. It picks up food like other plovers, tilting the body without flexing the legs. Insects form the major part of its diet but vegetable matter is also taken and when it occasionally resorts to the shore it eats molluscs and crustacea. Highly gregarious, large flocks collect in suitable areas throughout autumn and winter, breaking up in late February or early March. The young birds have short crests and pale edgings to the feathers, giving the folded wings a scaly look.

Voice A shrill, often wheezy-sounding 'pee-wit'. When displaying it has a longer-drawn-out 'per-weet-a-weet-weet' call, most frequently uttered in March and May.

Habitat In the breeding season, arable land, newly ploughed fields or fallow, moorland, rough ground, reservoir margins, sand and gravel workings, etc. At other times, the same but frequently more lowland areas.

Nest A scrape on open ground, with little or no lining but on occasions considerable addition of grasses and straw. Usually situated on a slightly raised area, mound or ridge between furrows of ploughed land. The 3 to 4 eggs are pear-shaped, stone-coloured, spotted and blotched with dark brown, laid late March or early April. One brood.

Status A resident and winter visitor. Breeds extensively throughout Britain and Ireland. Locally scarce in W Cornwall, Pembrokeshire, NW Scotland and SW Ireland. Estimated breeding population around 200,000 pairs, with many more present in winter.

Knot
Calidris canutus   W

Characteristics 10in (254mm). To see vast
flocks of wading birds in flight, appearing now
white and then black as they turn and wheel,
manoeuvring with extraordinary precision, is an
enthralling sight that can be witnessed from
autumn through to spring wherever these birds
congregate. Several species of wader perform in
such a manner, and after the Dunlin this bird is
the commonest on our estuaries and mudflats,
feeding between the tides on molluscs, crustacea
and worms. A plump medium-sized bird with a
short black bill and pale yellowish-green legs, the
Knot like most other waders has totally different
summer and winter dress, and during its moult
can show considerable variation between the two.
Frequently flocks contain birds in summer,
intermediate and winter plumage, which can be
confusing to the inexperienced observer. In
summer plumage the Knot has rufous-red
under-parts and a mixture of rich brown and
mauvish upper-parts. By late autumn it becomes
a nondescript greyish-looking bird with no real
distinguishing features other than size and shape,
though the greyish rump and its call note should
be sufficient to identify it.

Voice A low 'nut' when uttered by a flock has a

murmuring effect. In flight it has a whistling
'twit-twit' note.

Habitat Estuaries and mudflats. When inland it
frequents reservoir margins and similar watery
places.

Status A common passage migrant and winter
visitor, usually arriving late July to November
and leaving mid-March to mid-June. A number
of non-breeding birds sometimes occur during
the summer. Particularly abundant on the Wash,
Ribble and Dee estuaries. Total population
between 300,000 and 400,000 birds.

Sanderling
Calidris alba   W

Characteristics 8in (203mm). This active little
shore bird with its almost totally white plumage,
and short black bill and legs, is slightly larger than
the Dunlin with which it freely consorts. More
than any other wader the Sanderling is adept at
securing its prey from along the tide-edge, racing
after the retreating waves to take any small
crustacean, mollusc or worm that is revealed. It is
equally expert at dodging the oncoming breakers,
and spends a great deal of time feeding in this
manner. On other occasions it will race across the
sand on twinkling legs, stopping rapidly to probe
some suitable spot; or it will feed in soft sand well
away from water. It rarely congregates in such
great numbers as some other waders, but small
groups fly together, wheeling and turning with
equal precision. In flight there is a white wing bar
made more pronounced by a dark forewing. In
summer the head and breast are light chestnut,
rather sharply defined from the white belly, while
the brown and black back is not unlike the
Dunlin. In the autumn, moulting birds with odd
mixtures of winter and summer plumage can be
confusing.

Voice A short 'twick'.

Habitat A coastal species, preferring sandy
shores and flats. On migration regular in small
numbers at inland reservoirs, sand and gravel
pits, etc, particularly in spring.

Status A passage migrant and winter visitor. A
few non-breeding birds are present during
summer, the maximum number present in
Britain during autumn being probably around
30,000 birds.

Dunlin
Calidris alpina

Characteristics 6¾-7½in (171-190mm). This small wader is one of our commonest shore birds, but is often difficult to identify as it occurs at all times of year in a variety of plumage changes. However, when feeding it has a distinctive round-shouldered look as it probes for crustaceans and molluscs with a series of rapid movements of its bill as if 'stitching' the mud. Like many other shore birds it gathers in large flocks and performs spectacular aerial movements, wheeling and swerving in perfect unison. In summer it has a chestnut and black back with a black patch on the lower breast. In winter the back is grey-brown and the under-parts white, with some streaking on the breast, though it never looks as white as the Sanderling. Even the bill varies, being markedly longer and more curved towards the tip on some birds. There is a fairly noticeable wing bar and the white sides of the tail are apparent in flight.

Voice When feeding together, Dunlins keep up a low twittering chorus, but the individual alarm note and flight call is a long shrill 'tchurr'. The song is a rich purring trill, uttered in display flight or on the ground. Most frequently heard from May to July.

Habitat In the breeding season, typically moorland with tussocky grass, but also salt or fresh water marshes. Outside the breeding season, it frequents coastal areas of almost every type, particularly mudflats and sandy estuaries, and also goes inland, around lakes, reservoir margins, sand and gravel pits, river sides, etc.

Nest On the ground, a neat cup of grass, well hidden under a clump of grass or among heather, invariably near water. The eggs are bluish-green to brown, finely or thickly spotted or streaked in various shades of browns, laid in April to May. One brood.

Status Present all the year round. Breeding mainly in the Shetlands, Orkneys, NE Scotland and the Hebrides. Also along the Pennine chain, and in a few areas in Wales and on Dartmoor. In Ireland, found in central areas and the NW. Also scattered localities of Ulster. The total breeding population is 5,000 to 10,000 pairs. Also a passage migrant and winter visitor, occurring quite commonly inland. Probably half a million birds winter on main estuaries.

Similar or Allied Species Two races of Dunlin occur in Britain. The Southern Dunlin (*Calidris alpina schinzl*) which nests, is slightly smaller than the Northern Dunlin (*Calidris a. alpina*) which usually has a longer, more curved bill, and is mainly a winter visitor. The Little Stint (*Calidris minuta*) is much smaller than the Dunlin, with a short black bill and legs and a 'prit-a-prit' call note. A fairly scarce spring and autumn passage migrant. The Curlew Sandpiper (*Calidris ferruginea*) is longer in the leg than Dunlin, has a distinctive white rump and a 'chirrup' call note. A spring and autumn passage migrant in small numbers. The Purple Sandpiper (*Calidris maritima*) is a dark-looking wader, between Knot and Dunlin in size, with yellow legs and yellow base to the bill. A winter visitor, inconspicuously haunting rocky shores. Less active than other waders and does not gather in large flocks.

(left) Dunlin, summer plumage; (above) Curlew Sandpiper, winter plumage; (right) Dunlin, winter plumage

Ruff
Philomachus pugnax   J

Characteristics Male 11-12in (279-305mm).
Female 8½-10in (216-254mm). In breeding
plumage unmistakable, with an extensive frill
and tufts which can be black, brown, buff, white
or chestnut, or a combination of these. These
feather adornments are worn only by the male
and feature in its complicated ceremonial
displays, when great aggression is shown and
fighting between rival cock birds takes place at
the 'lek'. At the end of the breeding season the
male loses the frill and tufts, becoming less
distinctive and often a puzzle to the inexperienced observer. In flight, however
(which is heavy, with emphatic wing beats), an
oval white patch on each side of the dark central
area of the tail is a diagnostic feature. The bill is
medium length and slightly curved, the legs can
be orange-yellow, greenish or black. The female
Ruff or Reeve is somewhat smaller, as are the
juveniles in autumn, but the well-defined pattern
of black-brown feathers with buff edges is very
distinctive on these birds. The erect stance is also
characteristic and a more sedate way of feeding,
picking and probing for worms, molluscs and
insects, helps to distinguish it from other waders
such as the Redshank.

Voice Generally silent, rarely uttering a quiet
double-syllabled 'tu-wit' when put to flight.

Habitat In breeding season, low-lying wet
grassy meadows of fenland or marshy tracts. In
winter frequents marshes, sewage farms,
occasionally the coast.

Nest A hollow lined with fine grasses, usually
well hidden in marsh vegetation. The 4 eggs are
glossy, pale buff to pale green, bold spots and
blotches of dark brown concentrated at the large
end, somewhat like the Snipe's, laid in May. One
brood.

Status Present throughout the year. Some
breeding, but mainly a passage migrant regularly
noted inland. A few winter. It formerly bred in
Britain from Northumberland to SW England,
but declined in the last two centuries, finally
becoming extinct as a regular breeding bird until
recolonisation of the Ouse washes in 1963, where
up to 20 pairs now breed. A Schedule I bird.

Male, summer plumage

73

target for sportsmen, who regard it highly as a game bird. When coming in to land, it drops quite abruptly into cover, but occasionally the well-marked under-wing and greenish legs can be seen. A gregarious species, it is numerous at favoured feeding grounds, when wisps of a dozen or more might be seen flying round together. In spring it performs a remarkable diving display flight, the outer tail feathers vibrate rapidly to give a distinctive humming note which is termed drumming. On the breeding ground it perches on posts, fences and top branches of dead trees.

Voice When flushed a harsh 'scaap'. Spring song delivered from a post or fence is a monotonous 'chippa-chippa-chippa'.

Habitat In the breeding season, marshy areas, boggy moorland, sometimes dry heathery places. In winter it can be found in a wide variety of boggy marshy areas where it does not breed, frequenting sewage farms, floodwater, reservoir margins, stream sides, ditches, etc.

Status Present throughout the year, with large numbers arriving from NW Europe in the winter. Nests extensively in Britain and Ireland but sparse in SW Wales, SW England and central England. Total British and Irish population around 100,000 pairs.

Similar or Allied Species The Jack Snipe (*Lymnocryptes minimus*) is similar in appearance but smaller and darker looking with less distinctive stripings, and a much shorter bill. When flushed it does not zig-zag and settles after only flying a few yards. A winter visitor in small numbers, only occurring from August through to April.

Snipe
Gallinago gallinago

Characteristics 10½in (267mm). A secretive bird, adept at hiding from view in the marshy places it loves, where it probes deeply for worms with its long straight bill. Given a good view, the rich brown and black plumage strongly striped with golden yellow on the back, and the dark stripe through the eye and on the crown, are distinctive. It is more likely to be seen in flight, however, as it suddenly bursts from cover with a harsh call, zig-zagging away low over the ground before rapidly gaining height; it is a difficult

Common Snipe and (foreground) Jack Snipe

Woodcock
Scolopax rusticola

Characteristics 13½in (343mm). A rather solitary woodland species, most likely to be seen during the course of its 'roding' display flights; from March through to July, each dawn and dusk, the male traverses a variable circuit, flying quite fast, but with slow owl-like wing action, a little above the tree tops, frequently calling as it goes. On the ground it feeds as a Snipe does, probing deeply with its long straight bill, feeling for worms with its highly sensitive tip. When flushed from woodland cover it rises silently and with its bill held characteristically downwards, dodges through the trees with its twisting evasive flight. Much larger and stouter than a Snipe, its upper-parts are beautifully marked with rich brown, buffs and blacks, while the under-parts are finely barred with dark brown. When sitting on eggs this cryptic colouring renders the bird virtually invisible against a background of dead leaves and other woodland litter. Possibly only the large eye unusually positioned far back in the head might draw attention to its presence.

Voice When roding utters a low croaking sound. A thin 'tsiwick' note is uttered in both roding and non-roding flight.

Habitat Deciduous woodland with open rides, glades and good bracken cover, also wet areas for feeding.

Nest A shallow depression on woodland floor, lined with dead leaves. Often close to the base of a tree or fallen log, sometimes under brambles or under cover of bracken; on occasion in quite an open setting. The eggs are rounder than those of most wading birds, glossy, coloured from greyish-white to warm brown, spotted or streaked with darker brown. Laid in March to April. One brood.

Status Present throughout the year but with immigration of Continental birds in the autumn. Widely distributed as a breeding bird, but absent from a number of areas in England, particularly the Fens and parts of the SE and SW. Sparse or non-existent in western areas of Wales. Scarce in NW Scotland and not found in the Hebrides, the Orkneys or the Shetlands. Common in Ireland but missing from a good number of places there, particularly in the SW. Total breeding population of Britain and Ireland probably about 50,000 pairs.

75

Black-tailed Godwit
Limosa limosa

Characteristics 15-17in (381-432mm). A tall graceful-looking bird, frequently wading up to its belly to feed, often completely immersing the head. At other times it probes soft sand or mud with its long straight bill, searching for worms, molluscs and crustacea. In summer the head and breast are chestnut, the belly and flanks white with distinct black bars. The female, though similarly coloured, is duller looking. In winter both sexes look basically grey and white, but the flight pattern is always distinctive as the broad white wing bar, white tail with a broad terminal band of black and trailing legs identify it immediately. On its breeding ground it perches freely on fences and stumps, or trees and bushes where present. Generally it is only to be found in small groups, though flocks of several hundred can occur at favoured localities.

Voice A clear 'wicka-wicka-wicka-wicka' uttered by birds in flight.

Habitat In the breeding season it frequents reclaimed grassland, marshy areas, swamps or bogs. It winters on mudflats, salt marshes and estuaries, being less inclined to favour exposed shores. Also much more an inland bird, visiting fresh water marshes, lakes and reservoirs.

Nest A substantial pad of dead grasses, usually in a lush meadow or ley. The 4 eggs vary from pale blue-green to darkish brown, spotted or blotched with dark brown, laid in May. One brood.

Status Present throughout the year. Formerly it bred quite widely, becoming extinct as a breeding species in the mid-nineteenth century. Recolonisation began in the early 1950s in the Ouse washes, now the centre of the British population of around 50 breeding pairs. The total number wintering on the Exe and other SW coast estuaries is probably 5,000 birds. A Schedule I bird.

Similar or Allied Species The Bar-tailed Godwit (*Limosa lapponica*) lacks the Black-tailed Godwit's white bar, and has a barred tail; also the long bill is more upturned. In summer it is a rich chestnut-red about the head and neck, in winter grey-looking with mottled upper-parts. A passage migrant and winter visitor, generally distributed round all our coasts, particularly E and NW England and Scotland. Winter totals probably between 40,000 and 50,000 birds.

(left) Black-tailed Godwit; (right) Bar-tailed Godwit

Whimbrel
Numenius phaeopus

Characteristics 15-16in (381-406mm). An approachable 'Curlew' usually turns out to be a Whimbrel. Generally it is a much tamer bird than the Curlew which helps with identification as its boldly striped crown is not easy to determine at a distance, and unless a direct comparison can be made the smaller size and shorter curved bill are not by themselves sufficient to distinguish the two species. Even the flight pattern is similar, both having a white rump and no wing bar. However, the call is distinctive and once learned will indicate the bird's presence, for it can often be heard as it passes unseen overhead. As with the Curlew, the legs are greenish-grey and both sexes are similar. It feeds along the shore, often in the company of Curlew, probing for crustacea, molluscs and worms, though on its breeding grounds it also eats berries and insects.

Voice A rapid tittering 'titti-titti-titti-titti-tit' of even emphasis, often repeated seven times, hence a local name of Seven Whistler; it is also sometimes called the Titterel. The song is a bubbling trill similar to the Curlew's.

Habitat In the breeding season, moorland and heaths. Outside the breeding season, a coastal-haunting bird, but fond of fields and grasslands near coasts and also favours low rocky shores.

Nest A hollow among heather or other moorland vegetation, usually scantily lined with moss and heather. The 4 eggs are pear-shaped like the Curlew's, pale greenish to olive brown, blotched with dark brown, laid in May. One brood.

Status Summer resident and passage migrant. Breeds in the Shetlands, being relatively common in parts, but sparse in the Orkneys and the Outer Hebrides, with a few pairs found on the Scottish mainland. Total breeding population around 200 pairs. In other parts of Britain is mainly known as a bird of passage, particularly in the autumn: flocks can be seen moving south from late July through to October. A Schedule I bird.

Curlew
Numenius arquata

Characteristics 21-23in (533-584mm). Largest of the wading birds, and unmistakable, with a long down-curved bill and distinctive call. Gregarious and sociable at most times, it crowds together on mud banks and rocks, though frequently seen singly, especially in its moorland breeding habitat. A shy and wary bird it is difficult to approach on the open shore, but close to, the brownish plumage will be seen to be closely streaked with darker markings. The long legs are greenish-grey. The sexes are similar, though the female's bill is slightly longer. In flight, which is much slower than that of other waders and rather gull-like, it shows a barred tail and whitish rump extending to the lower back. When travelling any distance the flock usually fly high in long lines of V formation. On the coast it feeds with the tide, night and day, taking worms, molluscs and other marine invertebrates. On the moors its diet includes insects, worms and berries.

Voice Its 'cur-lee' cry gives the bird its name and is perhaps the best-known wader note there is, a far-reaching sound that can be heard at any time on its feeding or breeding grounds. The nuptial song flight, however, extends to a high-pitched bubbling trill, uttered by both sexes and regularly heard from February to July.

Habitat In the breeding season this is moorland, but it also nests in low-lying river valleys and water meadows. Outside the breeding season, mud flats, saltings, estuaries, also sandy and rocky shores, often resorting to grass and arable land at high tide. Frequent inland on migration.

Nest Usually a mere scrape in grass or heather, with little or no additional material. The eggs, usually 4, are pear-shaped, glossy, greenish to dark brown with speckles, blotches and streaks of brown, laid in April to May. One brood.

Status Resident, also a passage migrant and winter visitor. It nests extensively in the Orkneys, Shetlands and Scotland except NW, commonly in Wales and N England, southwards to Staffordshire. Also breeds in SE England westwards into Gloucester and Avon. Isolated breeding occurrences in other areas. Winter flocks around estuaries and mudflats probably total 250,000.

(left) Whimbrel; (right) Curlew

Redshank
Tringa totanus   S

Characteristics 11in (279mm). A noisy unapproachable bird; frequently dubbed 'warden of the marshes', it is invariably the first bird to take wing, calling in an almost hysterical manner when its territory is invaded. In flight it shows conspicuous white rear edges to the dark wings and a white back and rump, giving a very black and white appearance. On landing it noticeably holds its wings raised above its back for a moment or so, showing the very white under-wing. When observed close to, the rich brown upper-parts, head and neck are seen to be strongly streaked with black, the white under-parts closely streaked and speckled. In winter it loses its warm brown colouring and looks quite grey. At all times the long reddish bill, tipped with black, and the vermilion-red legs are distinctive, though legs of young birds are quite yellowish, as are adults' in winter. When suspicious, it rocks backwards and forwards on its legs. In the breeding season it perches freely on posts and branches of trees, from where it will call or launch itself on its aerial display flight, rising on quivering wings, accompanied by a long trilling call. When feeding, it probes and picks for molluscs, crustacea and worms, often wading up to its belly and swimming readily when out of its depth. It will also take vegetable matter, seeds and berries.

Voice A musical 'tuhu' and triple 'tu-hu-hu'. Also has a single alarm note, 'tcuk'. The song is a succession of sweet single notes uttered rapidly, culminating in a loud trill, regularly uttered from early March to June.

Habitat In the breeding season, grassy marshes, waterside meadows, margins of lakes and reservoirs, etc. At other times, tidal estuaries, mudflats and other suitable coastal areas.

Nest Hidden in deep grass, often with longer stems interlocked to form a canopy, but it can also be a scrape in dunes with only sparse marram-grass cover. The 4 eggs are whitish or creamy buff, spotted, streaked and blotched with shades of dark reddish-brown, laid April to May. One brood.

Status Present throughout the year, breeding regularly in many areas, particularly N England and Scotland but scarce or absent from NW Scotland. Scarce in Wales and SW England. Relatively uncommon in Ireland with main inland nesting sites centred on Connacht Lakes and Lough Neagh. Total British and Irish population around 50,000 pairs with probably as many again present in winter.

Similar or Allied Species The Spotted Redshank (*Tringa erythropus*) in summer plumage is sooty black speckled with white; in winter it looks more like the Redshank, but has no wing bar, has a longer thinner bill and its long legs project beyond its tail in flight. Its voice is a distinct 'tchu-wit'. A passage migrant in small numbers and occasionally winters.

(above) Redshank; (below) Spotted Redshank

79

Greenshank
Tringa nebularia

Characteristics 12in (305mm). The behaviour of this wary bird is similar in many ways to the Redshank's, but being slightly larger, taller and greyer-looking it should be easily identified, especially as (in good light) the legs are greenish. Also the slightly upturned thicker-looking bill is quite different, and is used to obtain food in several ways, including a side-to-side motion, sieving for small marine life, as well as for the more usual picking and probing for crustacea and molluscs. Quite frequently it will make a succession of rapid dashes through shallow water with the neck extended and bill submerged, chasing small fish and amphibians. When alarmed it will bob like the Redshank and is equally quick to take flight, usually calling as it does and revealing an extensive V of white up the back. The dark wings without any white bars are also distinctive. On its breeding ground it will perch freely on stone walls, fences or rocks, from where it will often sing.

Voice The usual note is a triple 'tchu-tchu-tchu'. The song is a rich fluty 'ru-tu, ru-tu, ru-tu' in display or ordinary flight and when at rest.

Habitat In the breeding season, treeless moorland with nearby lakes and rivers. Outside the breeding season, marshes, rivers, borders of lakes and reservoirs, salt marshes, estuaries, but it is less of a coastal bird than the Redshank.

Nest A scrape, lined with leaves, lichen, etc, frequently close to an outcrop of rock or piece of dead wood. The 4 eggs are buff to greenish, streaked and blotched or finely marked all over with reddish-brown, rather glossy, laid in May. One brood.

Status A resident and passage migrant. The British breeding population is confined to NE Scotland and the Hebrides. In a good year probably up to 750 pairs nest. There is only one recent nesting record from Ireland. Commonly noted on passage, particularly in autumn, frequently at suitable inland waters. A few birds over-winter. A Schedule I bird.

Common Sandpiper
Actitus hypoleucos

Characteristics 7¾in (197mm). This small wader is immediately identified by the constant up-and-down movement of its tail end, obvious as it perches on a rock or boulder in a stream or by a lake. Equally characteristic is the flight, usually a foot or so above the water, a regular, peculiar flickering wing beat and momentary glide on down-curved wings, an action unique to this bird. When disturbed it often flies out over the water, returning to shore in a wide arc, landing 100 yards (90m) or so from its starting point. A well-defined white wing bar, and white either side of the tail, are apparent when it takes wing; it invariably calls with a distinctive shrill note. Food is mainly obtained by picking rather than probing; it takes insects, worms, small molluscs and crustacea. In autumn the brownish plumage of the young birds is quite heavily barred.

Voice A far-carrying 'dee-dee-dee-dee'. The song, which has much the same quality as its normal call, is a 'kitti-wee wit, kitti-wee wit' uttered in flight or on the ground. Regularly heard from late April to early June.

Habitat In the breeding season, clear fast-running streams and borders of lochs, tarns and reservoirs in or close to hilly country, less frequently in lowland areas. Outside the breeding season, it frequents streams, rivers, reservoirs, sand and gravel pits, and occurs along estuaries, but rarely on the open shore or mudflats.

Nest Usually only a scrape, but frequently a fairly substantial cup of grass well hidden in vegetation, though occasionally quite exposed on a shingle river bank. The 4 eggs, whitish to yellowish-brown, are stippled, spotted, streaked or blotched with shades of red-brown, laid May to June. One brood.

Status A summer visitor, breeding widely in Wales, N England and Scotland where conditions are suitable. A scarce breeding bird in England south of a line from Humber to Severn. In Ireland it nests mainly in the eastern half of the country. Total breeding population around 50,000 pairs. Also a passage migrant (common) in spring and autumn with a small number over-wintering.

Similar or Allied Species The Green Sandpiper (*Tringa ochropus*) has a white rump and black under-wing. Its call is a distinctive 'klu-weeta-weeta'. Frequently noted on passage, especially in autumn; a few stay through the winter. Has also nested on occasions. The Wood Sandpiper (*Tringa glareola*) also has a white rump, but a grey under-wing, and calls 'chiff, chiff, chiff'. A few pairs nest in Scotland. Also a passage migrant in spring and particularly in autumn. Both Schedule I birds.

R.A.H.

(*above*) *Wood Sandpiper;* (*below*) *Green Sandpiper*

Turnstone
Arenaria interpres
S

Characteristics 9in (229mm). Unlikely to be confused with any other shore bird, as the adult male in summer plumage is a mixture of rich chestnut and black on the back with a bold pattern of black and white about the face and upper breast. The legs are orange-red and the bill is short, stout, pointed and black. The female has the same general appearance but is dingier-looking. As with other waders, the breeding plumage is replaced in winter by less distinctive colouring, but at all times its typical feeding behaviour is diagnostic, as it turns over small stones, seaweed and tideline debris in search of sandhoppers and other creatures. A pugnacious and quarrelsome bird, it rarely gathers in large flocks but often associates with Dunlin and other small waders. In flight it has a distinctive pied appearance with a lozenge-shaped white patch running almost the length of its back.

Voice A quick staccato 'tuc-a-tuc' and a long twittering trill.

Habitat Favours rocky, sea-weedy shores, also sandy and muddy flats where mussel beds are exposed or stony banks; found inland on migration, on the borders of lakes and reservoirs, by rivers and at sand and gravel pits.

Status Present throughout most of the year and widely distributed on suitable coasts, particularly in autumn. Many winter, and non-breeding birds are frequently observed through the summer. It has been suspected of breeding in Britain.

Red-necked Phalarope
Phalaropus lobatus ♂

Characteristics 7in (178mm). With its curiously lobed feet this tiny wader habitually swims, being rarely seen out of the water. A dainty bird, it can be absurdly tame, feeding almost at the feet of the observer. Summer dress is a combination of slate-grey on the head and shoulders with a bright orange patch down the side of the neck and white throat and under-parts. On the back are some buff streaks. In this species, the females are the more brightly coloured, the duller-looking males incubating the eggs and tending the young. In winter plumage it is pale blue-grey above, with white head and under-parts, but has a characteristic dark mark through the eye. Immature birds look similar but the upper-parts and crown are much darker. Feeding behaviour is most distinctive; when on shallow water it will spin, picking up food which is disturbed by the rotating movement of its body with a quick jab of its needle-fine bill.

Voice A shrill 'whit' or 'prit'.

Habitat In the breeding season, boggy areas with scattered pools and lagoons. On passage, frequents offshore waters and occasionally the coast. Inland it favours reservoirs, ponds and other shallow fresh waters. At other times it feeds far out at sea.

Nest A rather large scrape for the size of the bird, lined with grasses and other dry stems, usually well hidden in grass or other vegetation. It breeds in small groups, usually near the water. The eggs, pale green to buff, with heavy dark blotches and spots, are laid May to June. One brood.

Status A summer visitor, breeding in limited numbers in the Shetlands and Hebrides. Possibly declining. It formerly nested in Ireland. Quite a rare visitor to other parts of Britain, chiefly noted in autumn. A Schedule I bird.

Similar or Allied Species The Grey Phalarope (*Phalaropus fulicarius*) is quite distinctive in summer plumage, with dark chestnut under-parts, white face and dark crown. In winter it looks similar to the Red-necked Phalarope but the bill is shorter and thicker. It does not nest in Britain. It is frequently storm-driven, occurring offshore and also inland with greater frequency than the Red-necked Phalarope.

(above and centre) Grey Phalarope, winter and autumn plumage; (below) Red-necked Phalarope, autumn plumage

83

Arctic Skua
Stercorarius parasiticus

Characteristics 18in (457mm). This hawk-like sea bird is most likely to be seen as it pursues some luckless tern or gull in an attempt to rob it of its last meal. The Skua follows every twist and turn of the selected victim and invariably succeeds in forcing the bird to disgorge, or drop the fish it was carrying. It does, however, forage in typical gull manner, feeding on molluscs, crustacea, fish and carrion. On its breeding grounds small mammals, eggs, birds and insects are also taken. There are two distinct colour phases of this bird. In one, it has pale under-parts, in the other dark under-parts. In Britain the dark phase predominates, but many intermediates occur and in autumn immature birds further add to the difficulty of identification, particularly as their central tail feathers, a feature of the species, are not so distinct as in the adults. A fierce, parasitical bird, aggressive on its nesting ground, bold in defence of its territory, it swoops at intruders — animal and human alike — often culminating in a physical attack.

Voice On the breeding ground, a wailing, miaowing cry 'ka-aaaw' and variations.

Habitat In the breeding season, open moorland, heathy cliff tops, off-shore islands. The rest of the time at sea, often a great distance from land.

Nest A shallow scrape or hollow with little or no lining. Sociable nester, occurring in small colonies. The eggs vary from green to brown with dark brown spots and blotches, being laid in May to June. One brood.

Status A summer visitor, breeding in the Orkneys and Shetlands, the Hebrides and a few localities of the Scottish mainland. One of Britain's rarest breeding sea birds, with a total population of around 1,000 pairs. In autumn, particularly to be noted along the coast as it moves southwards on migration.

Similar or Allied Species Three other species of Skua occur in Britain. One, the Great Skua (Stercorarius skua), also breeds mainly in the Shetlands and Orkneys. The largest of the group, and dark brown with broad rounded wings with conspicuous white patches. It chases birds up to the size of the Gannet. The Pomarine Skua (Stercorarius pomarinus) has blunt twisted tail feathers and also occurs in dark and light forms. Much scarcer than the Arctic Skua, it does not nest in Britain. The Long-Tailed Skua (Stercorarius longicaudus) has a long tail but is much smaller than the Arctic Skua and has a distinctive dark cap contrasting with a broad-white collar. It does not nest in Britain; a rare passage bird.

*(above) a light-phase Arctic Skua pursues a Tern;
(below) Great Skua*

Black-headed Gull

Larus ridibundus

Characteristics 14-15in (356-381mm). The shape, form and generally white plumage of the gull family is familiar to everyone, and this species is particularly distinctive, certainly in the breeding season with its chocolate-brown hood, red bill and legs. In winter the head is white with only a dark smudge behind the eye. However, the broad white margin at the front of the narrow black-tipped wings is a distinctive feature at all ages and readily identifies this bird as it flies. The gull most frequently noted inland, it can be seen drifting in effortless flight over towns and cities, scavenging on rubbish dumps, squabbling over bread in park lakes, feeding on agricultural land where it follows the plough, roosting in large numbers on reservoirs. Around the coast it feeds as other gulls, but frequently plunge dives and occasionally tramples wet mud or sand to bring worms to the surface. Juvenile birds have a mottled brown back with a sub-terminal black band on the tail and pale orangey legs and bill.

Voice A noisy bird, especially on breeding grounds. Usual notes a harsh 'Kwarr' or 'kawup'.

Habitat In the breeding season, coastal areas, dunes, salt marshes, offshore islands, also inland marshes, edges of lakes. At other times it ranges far and wide but is less frequent along rocky coasts.

Nest Can vary from a mere scrape in the sand to a substantial structure of dead grass and reeds on the ground or in shallow water. Colonial, often in large numbers. The 2 to 3 eggs vary considerably in colour, from pale blue to greenish to deep-brown-blotched dark brown; often a clutch will contain a pale blue unmarked egg. Laid in April to May. One brood.

Status Present all the year round. Has the widest inland breeding distribution of the gulls and has increased considerably in numbers in recent years. Absent from rocky coasts and inshore islands of N and W Britain. Also sparse or absent as a breeding bird in S Wales, S and W England, and S and W Ireland. Total British and Irish population between 150,000 and 300,000 pairs.

In winter the dark head becomes white with a dark smudge behind the eye

Common Gull
Larus canus

Characteristics 16in (406mm). Similar in appearance to the Herring Gull but a smaller, longer-winged bird with a relatively slender bill (without any red spot) and greenish legs. When standing at rest the wings project much further beyond the tail, giving the body a more tapered look. In flight the white tips to the primaries are conspicuous, even more so when observed from below, providing immediate distinction between the same-sized Kittiwake, whose wing tips are wholly black. In winter the white head is streaked, giving it a dirty appearance. Immature birds have dark wing tips and trailing edge to the wing, with a broad black tail band, pink bill with a black tip, and yellow to flesh-coloured legs changing to blue-grey by the second winter. The Common Gull feeds in the usual scavenging manner of gulls and also drops molluscs like the Herring Gull. Sometimes chases Black-headed Gulls, forcing them to disgorge.

Voice A shrill whistling 'keeeyaa'.

Habitat In the breeding season, fresh water lochs, moorlands and hillsides, less often grassy cliffs or low offshore islands. Outside the breeding season, coastal areas, also inland, frequently arable and grassland. Appears to like playing-fields, also visits lakes, reservoirs and other inland waters.

Nest Sometimes just a scantily lined scrape, but sometimes a substantial platform of grass and seaweed. Can be found on rocky ledges or among vegetation, on shingle and burnt heather, etc, usually in small colonies. The 2 to 3 eggs are pale blue or green to dark olive, with brown blotches, spots and streaks, laid in May to June. One brood.

Status Present throughout the year. A common bird in Scotland, breeding widely northwards from the Solway. In England, the best-established breeding site is Dungeness, with only a few sporadic nesting occurrences elsewhere. In Ireland it is mainly found round the Ulster coast and the NW. Total British and Irish population around 50,000 pairs.

(left) Adult, winter plumage; (right) immature bird

Lesser Black-backed Gull
Larus fuscus

Characteristics 21in (533mm) The adult resembles the Great Black-backed Gull but is much smaller, about Herring Gull size, and has yellow legs — though these can be greyish or pinky in colour during winter. A further complication arises in that two distinct races of this bird occur in Britain. The British race, *Larus fuscus graselli*, has a slaty-grey back, the Scandinavian race, *Larus fuscus fuscus*, which is a passage migrant, a blackish back. The juvenile is very like the Herring Gull youngster, but the mottled brown plumage looks darker in some individuals though separation is not possible in every case. Adult plumage is assumed in the third or fourth year. Behaviour is similar to the Herring Gull's, and it feeds on the same wide variety of food, but is probably bolder and more aggressive.

Voice Various calls, like the Herring Gull's, but deeper in tone.

Habitat The same coastal preferences as the Herring Gull, but more frequent in offshore waters. In the breeding season, coastal dune systems or flat grassy slopes seem to be more generally favoured. Also nests more readily at inland sites.

Nest As Herring Gull on coast, but inland it uses heather, moss and lichen as well as grass. The nest is frequently sited among bracken or similar tall plants. The 2 or 3 eggs are indistinguishable from the Herring Gull's, laid April to May. One brood.

Status The British race is mainly a summer visitor, though some do winter. The major proportion of the breeding population is to be found in relatively few areas, with Walney Island (Lancashire) holding one-third of the British and Irish population, which the 1969-70 Operation Seafarer count put at 47,000 pairs. Increasingly common inland during the winter, feeding at rubbish tips and roosting on reservoirs. In 1963 around 6,000 were counted wintering at inland areas of England. By 1973 this had risen to over 17,000 and in the W Midlands it is numerically second only to the Black-headed Gull.

(left) British and (right) Scandinavian races

87

Herring Gull
Larus argentatus

Characteristics 22in (559mm). This typical 'seaside' bird is the commonest member of the gull family, frequenting holiday resorts, where it becomes fearless of man, taking food from the hand. Despite its quarrelsome greedy ways it is regarded with some affection, except perhaps by those who suffer from its recent roof-top nesting habits. In full plumage it is a most distinctive bird with pearly-grey back and white head and under-parts, flesh-coloured legs and a powerful yellow bill with a red spot on the lower mandible. The black-tipped wings have small white patches or 'mirrors'; these wear, however, and become less noticeable at times. As well as soliciting for food along the promenade, it follows ships, and haunts docks and quaysides, feeding on offal and scraps; it visits sewage outfalls and rubbish dumps and scavenges for anything edible. It drops shellfish to break them, tramples sand to bring up worms, eats carrion, young birds and eggs, as well as small rodents and insects. The immature birds are a dusky mottled brown, attaining adult plumage in their third year.

Voice A variety of mewing, barking and laughing notes, with a frequently repeated strident 'kyow'. Also has an anxiety call, 'yah-yah-yah'.

Habitat In the breeding season, cliff tops, low rocky islets, also coastal dunes and shingle, rarely salt marshes. Outside the breeding season, any coastal setting, also inland at rubbish tips, reservoirs, agricultural land, open areas, etc.

Nest Usually a large mound of grass, seaweed and other local debris, but sometimes only a meagre lined scrape in the sand or grass. The 2 or 3 eggs vary from pale blue to shades of green to dark brown, spotted and streaked very dark brown, laid in April to May. One brood.

Status Present throughout the year, breeding round most of coastal Britain except parts of NE England and East Anglia. Operation Seafarer found this bird to be the second most numerous gull with an estimated British and Irish population of 300,000 pairs.

Similar or Allied Species The Iceland Gull (*Larus glaucoides*) is a Herring Gull-sized 'white-winged gull'. It resembles the Glaucous Gull but is distinguished by a less heavy bill and at close range by a reddish eye-ring. Immature birds are pale creamy-brown. The Glaucous Gull (*Larus hyperboreus*) is sometimes as large as the Great Black-backed Gull. Adults have a pale grey back and pure white primaries, flesh-pink legs and a yellow bill with red spot. The yellow ring round the eyes is visible close to. Immature birds in their first year are pale creamy-brown.

Adult Herring Gull

Great Black-backed Gull
Larus marinus

Characteristics 25-27in (635-686mm). This huge, voracious gull dwarfs virtually every other shore bird and even without another species for comparison its great size is obvious. Further identifying features are the flesh-coloured or whitish legs and the black back; the British race of Lesser Black-backed Gull has a dark grey mantle. The flight is ponderous with slow deliberate wing beats, but at other times it sails effortlessly above the waves, frequently soaring to a great height. Its speed is deceptive, as it is fast and agile enough to chase other birds as a Skua does, forcing them to disgorge. It also kills both adult and young of other birds, particularly Puffins and Shearwaters. Rabbits and other mammals are also taken, as well as the more usual marine life, fish, crustacea and molluscs.

Voice A deep barking 'owk' and a guttural 'uk-uk-uk'

Habitat In the breeding season it favours the more rocky coasts and islands, though it sometimes nests on fresh water lochs some distance from the sea. At other times mudflats, estuaries, etc.

Nest A large pile of grass, heather, seaweed and other available material. Frequently sited prominently on a ridge or boulder, but sometimes on cliff slopes with other gulls. The 2 or 3 eggs are blotched with dark brown, laid in May. One brood.

Status Present throughout the year. Despite a marked increase since the turn of the century it is still the scarcest of established breeding gulls. Operation Seafarer put the total population in 1970 at 22,000 birds, over half of these in Scotland. In Britain it is an almost entirely west-coast breeding bird, from the Shetlands to Cornwall, but it is also found along the south coast, east to the Isle of Wight. In Ireland it occurs predominantly around west and southern coasts. It is noted more frequently inland than formerly, though still less often at any distance from the sea than any other of the commoner species of gull.

Kittiwake
Rissa tridactyla

Characteristics 16in (406mm). The adult Kittiwake generally resembles a Common Gull, but is slightly smaller and has solidly black tips to its wings, black legs and a yellow bill. The dark eye 'softens the expression', giving a less fierce appearance than other gulls have. Its more bounding flight with a quicker wing action also helps to separate it from other 'grey-backed gulls'. Food — small fish and other marine life — is taken by picking the surface in flight, or plunging in tern-like fashion, and sometimes by settling, then diving. It frequently follows ships. Juvenile Kittiwakes look different, showing a broad black collar across the back of the neck and a black diagonal band across the wing, giving a most distinctive flight pattern, like a black W.

Voice At its nesting area the 'kitti-waake' call which gives the bird its name is continuously heard, but at all other times it is mostly silent,

occasionally uttering a sharp 'kit-kit' when wrangling over food. The typical breeding-season call may, however, be heard at any time of year.

Habitat An oceanic species, frequenting offshore and pelagic waters. In the breeding season frequents rocky coasts where suitable cliff nest sites occur. Some birds, mostly immature, are occasionally recorded on passage at reservoirs and lakes in autumn and sometimes parties of adults in spring.

Nest Neatly constructed of grass and seaweed fixed to some rock projection or ledge, having a well-defined cup. The 2, sometimes 3, eggs are pale blue or greenish, blotched with dark brown or grey, laid end of May or early June. A colonial nester using precipitous sea cliffs; in recent years has also used buildings, such as riverside warehouses.

Status Present throughout the year, it breeds round most of Britain where suitable cliff nest sites occur, being mainly absent from, or sparse in, the greater part of E England and the S coast. Most large colonies are around Scottish coasts with concentrations in the Orkneys and Shetlands. Also breeds extensively around the Irish coast. As a breeding bird it has greatly increased in numbers this century. Operation Seafarer found an estimated total of 470,000 pairs nesting in Britain and Ireland.

Similar or Allied Species The immature Kittiwake is very similar to the juvenile Little Gull (*Larus minutus*), but its larger size and well-defined dark collar should identify it. It has nested. A Schedule I bird.

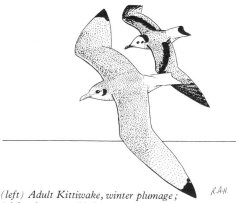

(left) Adult Kittiwake, winter plumage;
(right) immature bird

90

Sandwich Tern
Sterna sandvicensis

Characteristics 16in (406mm). The largest of our breeding terns. Its flight is less light and buoyant, its tail less deeply forked, than in others of this family. However, the long, narrow, pointed wings, black cap and longish black bill with yellow tip should prevent confusion with similar-sized gulls. When feeding it patrols inshore waters, hovering briefly, then plunging into the sea often from quite a height to secure a fish or sand eel, tending to stay submerged longer than other terns that feed in similar manner. When standing its black legs look comparatively long for a tern. It also displays a distinctive crest, particularly when excited. Winter plumage is assumed quite early (often while the birds are still breeding), the front of the crown turning white, until the head has a streaky appearance by September or October. Juveniles look similar to winter adults and can lack the yellow tip to the bill. Breeding colonies of these birds are easily disturbed, especially during the prospecting period, and will often quite suddenly desert an area.

Voice A noisy bird, calling frequently with a distinctive grating 'kirrick'.

Habitat Maritime, frequenting low-lying sandy or shingly beaches and sometimes rocky coasts or islands during the breeding season. It also nests on lakes a considerable distance from the sea in Ireland. Infrequent at inland waters on passage.

Nest A scrape or hollow with little or no lining, often on exposed sand but sometimes hidden in marram grass. Colonial, nesting much closer together than other terns. The 1 or 2 eggs are white, cream or brown with streaks, spots, blotches or reddish-brown smears, much larger than those of other terns, and laid in May. One brood.

Status A summer visitor, first arrivals noted in early March, departing September to October. Colonies are scattered around the coast at suitable localities with numbers fluctuating and sites often changed. British and Irish population probably around 15,000 pairs.

Winter plumage

Common Tern

Sterna hirundo   S

Characteristics 14in (356mm). A slender graceful medium-sized bird, with white underparts, pale grey back, black cap, red legs and red, black-tipped bill. The long pointed wings and forked tail with projecting streamers give the name Sea Swallow, though it has no relationship with *Hirundo rustica*. The Arctic Tern is similar in appearance and the two are easily confused. At close range the scarlet bill with its black tip identifies the Common Tern, but this clue is only reliable in the breeding season; in the early part of the year the Arctic Tern can still have a black-tipped bill (wholly blood-red in the summer). In winter, too, its black cap is incomplete, and both Arctic and Common Tern show a white forehead. At rest, differences are more conspicuous when the birds are seen side by side; for example, the folded wings of the Common Tern are the same length as the tail, while the Arctic Tern's tail extends well beyond the folded wing. Also the Arctic Tern's legs are noticeably shorter. In flight the innermost primary feathers of the Common Tern when seen from below show up as a translucent panel or 'window', whereas all are translucent on the Arctic. The upper wing has darker streaking near the tip on the Common Tern but is clear pale grey on the Arctic. Young birds show darker shoulder patches than young Arctic Terns. The Common Tern feeds on small fish and sand eels, flying methodically above the water, plunging in to secure prey.

Voice Extremely noisy on breeding grounds. The usual call is a long grating 'keeeee-yaah', also a frequently uttered 'kik-kik-kik'.

Habitat In the breeding season, inshore waters of low-lying coasts and islands with dunes or salt marshes. Also breeds along rivers, lakes and sand and gravel pits. On passage, regular at inland waters.

Nest A scrape on sand or shingle, sometimes on dried mud or turf with varying amounts of local material, grasses, etc, added. It is a colonial nester, often in considerable numbers, though occasionally solitary. The 2 to 4 eggs vary from cream to dark brown, also pale green and blue, with spots and blotches of dark brown, laid in May. One brood.

Status A summer visitor, arriving April departing October. A widely distributed breeding tern, the majority found along W coast of Scotland. In England it is concentrated along the Norfolk, Suffolk and Essex coastline, also Hampshire and Dorset. A fair number breed inland in NE Scotland and some in the E Midlands of England. Breeds on Anglesey, Isle of Man and Isles of Scilly. In Ireland it is found at suitable localities around the coast, also inland particularly in NE. Total breeding population around 20,000 pairs.

(left) Adult and (right) juvenile, both in winter plumage

Arctic Tern
Sterna paradisaea

Characteristics 15in (381mm). Similar to the Common Tern, but its more buoyant airy flight, with its longer streamers and relatively slimmer wings, is readily noted. More subtle differences, such as the greyer-looking under-parts, are detected with experience. The wholly blood-red bill, which is generally shorter than the Common Tern's black-tipped bill, remains a useful distinguishing feature, certainly in the breeding season. The extremely short legs can provide a means of identification when the observer is familiar with the longer-legged Common Tern, though that species can at times adopt a squatting stance giving a short-legged effect. The Arctic Tern's behaviour is little different from the Common Tern's, but it is possibly more aggressive on breeding grounds, pressing home its aerial attacks more vehemently when an intruder invades its nesting territory and it will draw blood from the unprotected head of a trespassing human. It feeds on fish in the same manner as other terns. The diet also includes crustacea, molluscs and some insects.

Voice A high whistling 'kee-kee' rising in pitch and notes similar to the Common Tern.

Habitat Similar to the Common Tern's, but more maritime and less inclined to nest away from the coast. Quite frequent at inland waters on passage.

Nest Usually only a scrape on sand, shingle or turf, lined with marram grasses, shells, etc,

occasionally ringed with stones. A colonial nester, frequently with Common Terns. The 1 to 3 eggs are indistinguishable from the Common Tern's, laid in May. One brood.

Status A summer visitor and passage migrant, arriving April to May, leaving August to October. Our most numerous nesting tern, with its stronghold in N and W Scotland. Estimates put the British and Irish population at between 40,000 and 50,000 pairs.

Similar or Allied Species The Roseate Tern (*Sterna dougallii*) has very long tail streamers and looks much whiter, with relatively shorter wings. Its breast is flushed with pink in summer. The bill is mostly black. It has a characteristic 'chy-ick' call. It occurs with Common and Arctic Terns but is much scarcer. The total population at the handful of breeding colonies in Britain and Ireland is probably about 875 pairs and the total in NW Europe is under 1000. A Schedule I bird.

(above) Arctic Tern; (below) Roseate Tern

Little Tern
Sterna albifrons

Characteristics 9½in (241mm). Smallest of the sea terns, it flies with much quicker movements, and when feeding it hovers on rapidly beating wings before plunging into the water to secure some small fish. With its white forehead, black-tipped yellow bill and yellow feet, it is comparatively easy to identify in the breeding season, compared to others in this group. In winter and juvenile plumage it is much like the Common Tern, but always distinguishable by the size and by bill and foot colour. In juveniles the bill and foot colour is much duller. Less gregarious than other terns, it is rarely seen in any great numbers.

Voice A harsh rasping 'kyik', a sharp repeated 'kitt' and a rapid chattering 'kirri-kirri-kirri-kikki'.

Habitat During the breeding season, sandy and shingle beaches. On passage it is occasionally noted at inland waters.

Nest A scrape on the sand or shingle. No material is used, though sometimes small pebbles form a lining. Usually it nests in small colonies of half a dozen pairs or so, strung along the same contour line of beach, several yards apart. The 2 or 3 eggs are pale stone, bluish or brownish, spotted with light brown, laid in May. One brood.

Status A summer visitor, breeding in suitable areas. It has decreased markedly in recent years, with human disturbance a major cause. The present population is put at around 1,800 pairs, concentrated around the coast of East Anglia and SE England. A Schedule I bird.

R.A.H.

94

Guillemot

Uria aalge S

Characteristics 16½in (419mm). This bird and the Razorbill and Puffin are our commonest breeding auks, all basically black and white sea birds nesting on sea cliffs or in holes. The Guillemot and Puffin are the most numerous, the former distinguished from the Razorbill, which it superficially resembles, by a slender pointed bill and thinner neck; also when observed at close range, by its brown, not black, upper-parts, especially the head. However, birds of more northerly areas can have bodies almost as black as the Razorbill's. There is also a 'bridled' form, which has a white ring round the eye and a white line running back from it over the sides of the head. This variety comprises about 1 per cent of the population in S and SW England, increasing northwards to about 25 per cent in the Shetlands. In winter, the side of the head and throat are white but with a conspicuous black line from the eye across the ear coverts. On the water it swims buoyantly, diving to catch fish which it swallows below the surface, often staying under for over a minute. Flight is fast and direct, to and from feeding grounds to the nest site, skimming near to the surface on thin, narrow, rapidly beating wings. On cliff ledges it perches in an upright position looking penguin-like.

Voice Very noisy at the nest site, giving a prolonged growling 'arr'; at breeding colony emits a considerable din.

Habitat In the breeding season, sea cliffs with ledges and flat-topped stacks. Outside breeding season, well out to sea. Only comes inland when storm-driven.

Nest In colonies on cliff ledges, often in company with Razorbills, Kittiwakes and Puffins. No material is used. The 1 egg is laid direct on bare rock, and is large and pyriform, having endless colour variations from deep blue-green to buff, sometimes red with brown and black spots, blotches and a tracery of black lines; laid in May. One brood.

Status Present throughout the year with a basically west-coast distribution where suitable cliffs occur. It leaves the nest site in early August, returning late December to early February. In 1969-70 Operation Seafarer found the total British and Irish population to be over half a million pairs, 80 per cent of these in Scotland and the biggest colonies in the Orkneys.

Winter plumage

Razorbill

Alca torda   S

Characteristics 16in (406mm). When seen at a distance it always looks much blacker than the Guillemot, while at close range the laterally compressed bill crossed by a white line is a distinctive feature. On the water it is more compact and plumper than the Guillemot, having a thicker neck and heavier-looking head. The tail is also longer and pointed and often cocked. In winter it has a white face. It dives for fish with more of a splash than other auks, giving a distinct kick of the legs and flick of partly opened wings as it does so. Dives tend to be shorter than the Guillemot's. Flight is similar to that of the Guillemot and the two species are almost impossible to separate when the different shape of the bill is not discernible, especially in winter. It is as gregarious as the Guillemot and the two are usually found together, though small groups of the one species are met on occasions, and unusually one bird on its own.

Voice At breeding grounds a prolonged grating, growling 'caarr'; also a tremulous whirring sound.

Habitat Similar to the Guillemot's.

Nest Usually in some recess, hole or crack in rock, but sometimes in the open. Less dependent on steep cliffs, it will nest among rocks and boulders along the shore. No nest material. The one egg is more conical than the Guillemot's and though showing considerable variation is rather more of a regular type; its ground colour may be creamy white, blue-green or brown with spots, streaks and blotches; laid in May. One brood.

Status Present throughout the year. At nesting sites from March to August, generally distributed at sea during the other months. Probably 70 per cent of the world's population nest in Britain and Ireland. It has a west coast distribution from the Shetlands southwards to Cornwall, and is also mainly located at west-coast sites in Ireland. Apart from Bempton Cliffs (Yorkshire), it is absent from most of E and S England, reflecting a lack of suitable nest sites. Total population was estimated at 144,000 pairs in 1969-70.

Winter plumage

Black Guillemot

Cepphus grylle   S

Characteristics 13½in (343mm). Unmistakable in summer with its uniformly black
plumage and conspicuous white wing
patches, this handsome bird is slightly smaller
than the Razorbill, with which it rarely
associates. At close quarters the bright red feet
can be seen and, when calling, the brilliant
vermilion gape. In flight it is even more striking,
the all-black body contrasting with a white
under-wing bordered with black, like no other
sea bird. In winter the under-parts are white
and the dark upper-parts mottled with white.
Adults can be identified by their red feet, while
juveniles' feet are yellowish and the gape orange.
The Tystie, as it is sometimes called — a name
derived from the Norse — swims and dives
with the same alacrity as other auks, but
probably stays submerged somewhat longer as it
seeks small fish, molluscs and crustacea. Some
seaweed is also taken. Usually to be found singly
or in small groups, and tends to keep more to
inshore water than other auks.

Voice A shrill whistling 'peeeee', sometimes
developing into a trilling twitter when the
distinctive gape is most noticeable.

Habitat In the breeding season, the sea coast
and islands with rock or boulder-strewn shores.
At other times, inshore water. Rarely inland.

Nest No material is used, and usually in a hole or
crevice, under a boulder, etc. 1 or 2 eggs, whitish,
pale blue-green and buff, spotted or blotched
with dark reddish-brown or black, laid in May to
June. One brood.

Status A resident, breeds in the Shetlands, the
Orkneys, the Hebrides and the W coast of
Scotland southwards to the Solway. Also in the
Isle of Man and Anglesey. Found at scattered
localities round the Irish coast, mainly in the
west. The first census made of this species was in
1969-70 when Operation Seafarer established a
breeding population of 8,340 pairs.

*(above left and foreground) Summer plumage;
(above right) winter plumage*

97

Puffin
Fratercula arctica S

Characteristics 12in (305mm). Certainly the most popular of sea birds and probably the best-known member of the auk family, this species is remarkable for its colourful parrot-like beak, which gives it that comical appearance. The beak is in fact well adapted to holding its prey: individuals can often be seen returning to their nesting burrows carrying several sand eels at a time. After the breeding season the basal part of the bill covering is shed, giving a more angular appearance and the bill becoming mainly yellow in colour. At their breeding places Puffins are usually quite tame, and may be watched at close range; it can then be noted that their quaint appearance is not only due to the unique bill-shape, which gives rise to such local names as Sea Parrot or Coulterneb, but also to the deep-set eye positioned above the full round cheek from which a conspicuous groove curves backwards. Also note the crimson ring round the eye and blue wattles above and below it. The bird stands very upright on the full length of the leg, walking with a rolling gait and also running quite quickly. The flight is rapid. On the sea Puffins occur in huge 'rafts', at home in the wildest conditions, riding the waves with ease.

Voice A low growling 'arr'.

Habitat In breeding season, turfy islands or cliff tops. At other times, frequents offshore waters, but also found well out at sea.

Nest In an underground burrow excavated by the bird itself or by rabbits. Sometimes in cracks in rocks or holes in cliffs, with a lining of dry grass and feathers. The single egg (sometimes 2) is white with traces of markings below the surface, laid in May. One brood.

Status Present throughout the year. Main concentrations found in the Orkneys and Shetlands, also western islands of Scotland. Other colonies scattered around coasts of western Britain and Ireland. Has declined markedly in recent years. Present population around 500,000 pairs.

Similar or Allied Species The Little Auk (*Plantus alle*) is a black and white sea bird, much smaller than the Puffin. It has a very short bill and neckless appearance, and flies very fast over the sea. A winter visitor, it is most often seen when driven towards shore by strong winds; sometimes occurs far inland after severe gales.

Puffin

Stock Dove
Columba oenas

Characteristics 13in (330mm). When feeding on the ground this generally grey-looking bird is easily overlooked, for it lacks any eye-catching features: only at close quarters can the iridescent green patch on the neck and vinous-coloured breast be seen. In flight, however, the pale blue-grey wings with their black borders and the black terminal band on the tail distinguish it from other pigeons. A gregarious bird, its habits are similar to the Wood Pigeon's, though it is rarely met in large numbers and its habitat preference is somewhat different. Young birds are fed on regurgitated food, known as 'pigeon's milk'.

Voice A deep 'ooo-woo', the second syllable short and emphatic. Calls regularly from February onwards with a break in August, less frequently heard at other times.

Habitat Woodlands, parklands with old timber, but also the vicinity of sea cliffs and rocky places, sand dunes, etc. Also frequents ruins, old castles and the like. Feeds in fields and open ground.

Nest The only European pigeon to nest in holes or cavities, which can be in a tree or building, outcrop of rock or rabbit burrow. Little or no nesting material is added to the scrape on the hole floor. Eggs, usually 2, are pure white, more pointed and less glossy than the Wood Pigeon's, laid March onwards, through to September. Two broods, sometimes three.

Status A resident, widely distributed except for the major part of N Scotland, the Hebrides, Orkneys and Shetlands. Scarce or absent in parts of Ireland particularly the NE. Following a general expansion in the nineteenth century, has decreased locally since the mid-1950s. Total British and Irish population estimated at around 100,000 pairs.

Wood Pigeon
Columba palumbus

Characteristics 16in (406mm). The largest of our pigeons, this is a very noticeable and familiar bird, sometimes occurring in huge flocks, especially in the winter when it does great damage to vegetable crops, feeding extensively on grain, peas, beans, seeds, etc. Even at a distance the plump body and small head are distinctive, while at close range the vinous-coloured upper breast and the glossy green and purple neck-markings with a white patch each side readily distinguish it from the Stock Dove. (Juvenile birds lack the neck markings.) When flushed it rises with a clatter of wings, showing prominent white wing flashes and a broad dark terminal band on the tail. Often shy and wary it is a swift and capable flyer, but in areas where it is not persecuted it will become quite tame and freely mixes with feral pigeons, feeding unconcernedly in town parks and other open spaces. Pigeons feed their young on 'pigeon's milk', a highly nutritious fluid manufactured in the crop, which allows the species to breed during most months of the year.

Voice A regular repeated five-note sequence of 'coo-coooo-coo, coo-coo'. It calls at most times throughout the year but with great frequency between February and September.

Habitat Well-wooded countryside and agricultural land. Also frequents town parks and city suburbs with plenty of tree cover.

Nest A lattice of small twigs lined with rootlets, grass or straw, often on foundation of previous nest. Usually in a bush or tree, a foot or two (½-

1m) off the ground upwards to 40ft (10-15m). Eggs, usually 2, are white and glossy, laid as early as February, through to October. Two broods are usual.

Status Present throughout the year, being widely distributed and breeding in all areas of Britain and Ireland except extreme N of Scottish mainland and Shetland. Total population around 5 million pairs.

Similar or Allied Species Feral and town pigeons, such a feature of city centres, are descended from escaped or stray domestic pigeons and show a variety of plumages, though some have a white rump and two black bands across the wings much like the wild Rock Dove, ancestor of the domestic pigeon. Few truly wild Rock Doves (*Columba livia*) are now to be found, but some still breed along the more remote rocky coasts of Scotland and Ireland. Feral pigeons also haunt rocky coasts.

Wood Pigeon

Collared Dove
Streptopelia decaocto

Characteristics 11in (279mm). Though sometimes confused with the Turtle Dove, this bird is much less colourful. It has a pale, dusty-brown appearance with a narrow black half-collar at the back of the neck. Juveniles are much greyer looking and lack the collar. In flight, the brownish back and pale grey secondaries and coverts contrast with the dark primaries; yet when viewed from below it is a nondescript-looking bird except for the black tail with its broad white terminal band, a conspicuous feature when expanded. As all European pigeons and doves, this species is granivorous and noteworthy concentrations occur where grain is handled or processed. It is as shy and wary as the Wood Pigeon even though it is more a bird of the suburbs, frequenting habitations, often to be seen perching on television aerials. When coming in to land it approaches with a series of characteristic hesitant checks and starts.

Voice A deep 'coo-coooo-cuk' with emphasis on the second syllable. Also has a frequently uttered flight call, a throaty 'kwurr'.

Habitat A bird of town suburbs and villages. Also frequents farm granaries and docks where grain is handled.

Nest A frail platform of fine twigs lined with grasses. Has been recorded building its nest totally of wire scraps. Preferred sites are in conifers or yew, but thick bushes or hedges are often used and occasionally buildings. Two eggs, white, glossier than those of the Turtle Dove. Breeds from February to November, raising two or three broods.

Status In Britain the Collared Dove first nested near Cromer, Norfolk, in 1955. Ten years later the population had increased to nearly 20,000 birds and it is still increasing, though beginning to stabilise at around 40,000 to 50,000 pairs. Mainly absent from higher regions of Britain and central areas of Ireland.

101

Turtle Dove
Streptopelia turtur

Characteristics 11in (279mm). Perhaps the most colourful of our doves. (Smaller members of the *Columbidae* are usually called doves, the larger species being generally referred to as pigeons.) This species is distinguished by the boldly patterned rufous and black back, pale grey head with black and white striped patch on the side of the neck, and soft pinkish throat and breast. The long graduated tail is black with a broad white band which is most noticeable in flight. Juveniles lack the black and white neck patch and pinky breast colour. Habits differ little from those of other pigeons, but Turtle Doves are less gregarious and are usually only found in ones and twos, though in late summer small groups occasionally collect at favoured feeding areas. Frequently perches on telegraph wires. Fumitory forms a major part of the diet but various seeds of other kinds are also eaten.

Voice A monotonous purring 'rroorrrr-rroorrrr-rroorrrr' which can be heard regularly from late April to July and less frequently in August.

Habitat Open woodlands, park land, large gardens, open country with tall hedgerows.

Nest A flimsy platform of fine twigs, lined with fine roots and grasses. Typically sited in a hawthorn hedge but also frequently in a bushy woodland tree. The 2 eggs are white and glossy. Laid mid-May onwards. Two broods.

Status A summer visitor, generally arriving mid-April, leaving July-August, though often some birds are still around in September. Has increased slightly in recent years, found mainly from Yorkshire and Lancashire southwards, and there are a few records of nesting in Scotland, though absent from W Wales and parts of Devon and Cornwall. Only the occasional breeding record from Ireland. Total British population probably about 125,000 pairs.

Cuckoo
Cuculus canorus

Characteristics 13in (330mm). Probably no other bird is so well known by reputation or by voice. In flight it could be mistaken for a Sparrowhawk, though the pointed wings and graduated white-spotted tail should distinguish it. When seen perched, the blue-grey upper-parts and whitish under-parts with dark barring on the lower breast are further distinguishing features, and the pointed bill is not that of a raptor. The distinctive call is unmistakable and when delivering it from the branch of a tree or post the bird has the habit of raising its tail and dropping its wings. In early spring it repeats the call when chasing. Nuptial flights of two or three males and females can be observed when the entirely different note of the hen bird can be heard, but otherwise there is no immediate difference between the sexes. The juvenile is rufous-brown, strongly barred with black, superficially resembling a Kestrel. There is a rare colour phase in the adult female, which then looks like the juvenile. An insectivorous bird, particularly fond of caterpillars.

Voice The usual 'cuc-koo' with variants can be heard from April to May and in June, when a change in tune can be noted. There is also a harsh laughing alarm note, a deep 'kow-kow-kow' common to both sexes. The female also has a long bubbling call.

Habitat Virtually any type of countryside.

Nest Parasitic, laying eggs in the nest of a victim which it locates by watching the bird build. Dunnock, Robin, Pied Wagtail, Reed Warbler and Meadow Pipit are especially favoured, though over 50 species have been recorded as host. Study has shown that the female lays as many as 12 eggs, sometimes more, in different nests, usually favouring one species. The eggs tend to resemble the foster parents', but are sometimes larger. The young cuckoo when hatched heaves out other eggs or young birds.

Status A summer visitor arriving in April, adults leaving July to August juveniles August to September. Generally distributed and common in some areas, since the early 1950s it has suffered a slight decline, particularly in E counties. The population of Britain and Ireland is estimated at 60,000 birds.

typical round flat owl-face with large dark eyes, and the long legs, are very apparent. Considered to be a beneficial species, feeding mainly on rodents, it sometimes takes small birds and occasionally insects, frogs and fish. It ejects distinctive shiny black pellets which can be found on the floor where it nests or roosts.

Voice An eerie long-drawn shriek often given in flight is the most frequently uttered note, for which reason it is sometimes known as the Screech Owl. At the nest site old and young birds alike make hissing, yapping and snoring noises.

Habitat Closely associated with man, haunting the vicinity of old buildings, church towers, barns, ruins, etc, hunting over fields and open country. Also found in wilder country well away from human habitation, including marshland.

Nest In old ruins, barn lofts, holes in trees, where it lays 4 to 7 white eggs (more pointed than those of other owls) on floor debris, usually April or May. Frequently two broods.

Status A resident, generally distributed, but quite scarce in many areas. Breeds rarely in NW Scotland and is virtually unknown in the Outer Hebrides, Orkneys and Shetlands. Absent from parts of Ireland. Estimated population of Britain and Ireland around 10,000 pairs. A Schedule I bird.

Similar or Allied Species The Snowy Owl (*Nyctea scandiaca*) is a very large, predominantly white bird. The female is quite heavily barred on the upper-parts. Has bred in recent years in Shetlands, but otherwise is an extremely rare winter visitor. A Schedule I bird.

Barn Owl
Tyto alba

Characteristics 14in (356mm). With its ghostly white form and association with churchyards and old ruins, it is little wonder this bird has become linked with tales of the supernatural. It usually becomes active at dusk, when it quarters low over the ground with a slow, buoyant, wavering flight alternating with short glides. Sometimes it hunts in daylight, when its beautiful orange-buff and vermiculated upper-parts can be seen more easily. When perched, the

Barn Owl

Little Owl
Athene noctua

Characteristics 8½in (216mm). A small, plump, compact bird with flat head and short tail. Its greyish-brown plumage, spotted, mottled and barred with white, provides a distinctive combination of markings, enabling quick identification. Additionally, the facial discs are flattened above the yellow eyes, giving a fierce frowning expression. More diurnal than other owls, it can sometimes be seen perched on a telegraph pole or tree branch in broad daylight, when it is often mobbed by small birds. It also favours gates and posts, where it will sit in an upright position. When alarmed it 'bobs' in a Robin-like fashion. Flight is undulating, recalling a woodpecker, though its rounded wings and general appearance proclaim its identity. It feeds mainly on insects, large beetles and worms, but will take small birds, small mammals and reptiles.

Voice Usual note is a monotonous and rather plaintive 'kiew', a bit like a Lapwing's peewit call, but shorter. It has other less frequently used barking notes.

Habitat Agricultural land with plenty of trees and farm buildings, parkland, also industrial wasteland, moorland edges and coastal areas.

Nest Usually a hole in a tree, but frequently in a building, sometimes a rabbit burrow or other cavity. No nest material used. The eggs, 3 to 5, are matt white, elliptical, laid in late April to May. Single-brooded.

Status Introduced into Britain during the nineteenth century, when first attempts in Yorkshire were unsuccessful. Extensive introductions near Oundle (Northamptonshire) around 1890 resulted in established breeding in the area and it subsequently spread to nearby counties. By the early part of the twentieth century the Little Owl had extended its range to most of the Midlands and S England. There have been some decreases in recent times but it continues to spread slowly northwards. Rarely noted in Scotland and Ireland. Estimated population around 10,000 pairs.

R.A.H.

Tawny Owl
Strix aluco

Characteristics 15in (381mm). The hoot of an owl is one of the most easily recognisable sounds of nature and familiar to most people, but not everyone realises that the originator of this call is the Brown Owl — or the Wood Owl as the Tawny is also sometimes known. Thoroughly nocturnal, it roosts by day in a hollow tree or thick bush (often holly) providing little chance for observation. If disturbed during the daytime, or perhaps seen on the wing at dusk, it appears as a moderately large bird with short rounded wings and large head. When viewed at close quarters the rich mottled brown plumage and conspicuous white patches on the wings can also be seen. Prey is mostly taken from the ground and includes mammals, especially field mice, field voles and shrews. Some birds are also taken, principally Starlings and Sparrows, but other species up to the size of Stock Dove and Green Woodpecker have been recorded. It has also been known to kill Barn Owls, possibly in competition for nest sites. Fish are not infrequent prey, with the occasional frog or newt, and quite often worms are brought to the nest. It ejects pellets of undigested material, as other owls, but not at the nest site as the Barn Owl does. There is a grey phase of this bird, but it is rare in Britain.

Voice A prolonged trisyllabic 'hoo-hoo-hoo' followed by a long-drawn-out quivering 'hoooooooo'. Regularly heard from mid-January to June and less frequently at other times. Calls occasionally before dusk. Also has a distinctive 'ker-wick' note uttered in flight.

Habitat Woodland, farms, parks and frequently suburban areas where there are plenty of trees. Rarely in more open country.

Nest Usually in a hole in a tree, sometimes in an old squirrel's drey or Crow's nest. Will use nest box (barrel or owl chimney). Rarely nests on the ground. No nest material used. The eggs, 2 to 4, are glossy white, often laid in early March. One brood. Like all owls it begins incubation immediately after the first egg is laid, so that the young birds grow at different rates.

Status Resident, generally distributed throughout Britain but rare in NW Scotland. Unknown in the Hebrides, and also absent from the Orkneys and Shetlands and from Ireland. Estimated population 100,000 pairs.

Long-eared Owl
Asio otus

Characteristics 13½in (343mm). Most nocturnal of the owls, seldom noted by day unless found roosting, when in an effort to remain undetected it presses itself against the trunk of a tree and then has a long thin look. In a relaxed posture it has a more squat rounded appearance and might be mistaken for a Tawny Owl, but the ear tufts (they are not its true ears) and orange-yellow eyes are always distinctive. The upperparts are a beautifully marked mixture of brown and black with vermiculated greyish-buff and dark brown, the breast delicately streaked dark brown with wavy transverse barring, visible at close quarters. When seen in flight it looks greyer than the Short-eared Owl, its long wings also ruling out the Tawny Owl, though the ear tufts lie flat and cannot be seen. Its prey includes small mammals, but can vary in some instances, being predominantly small birds, which are often taken as they roost, with a pair operating together, one flushing, the other catching.

Voice A low moaning 'oo-oo-oo-oo' uttered at regular intervals. Heard mainly in spring, being generally silent after nesting is completed.

Habitat Mainly coniferous woodland and forestry plantations, but it also occurs in small belts or isolated stands of trees. Where common it is found in deciduous woodland. It also hunts over open country.

Nest It uses the old nest of another bird, such as Sparrowhawk, Carrion Crow or Magpie; sometimes nests on the ground. The 3 to 6 eggs are white and elliptical, laid March to April. One brood.

Status A resident, also a winter visitor. It has a scattered distribution, being scarce or unknown in many areas, particularly the Midlands, SW England, parts of NE England, Wales and NW Scotland. Fairly common in Ireland where it replaces the Tawny Owl. Total British and Irish population probably not over 10,000 pairs.

RAH.

Short-eared Owl
Asio flammeus

Characteristics 14½-15in (368-381mm). Though most active at dusk, this owl hunts in daylight more than other owls, and when observed its frequent wheeling and gliding on long soft wings might at first suggest some diurnal bird of prey. However, the typical facial disc of an owl is readily detected and at really close range the distinctive yellow eyes can be seen. The upper-parts appear marbled in buffs and dark browns, the short tail and the wings are distinctly barred. A dark carpal patch is noticeable on a pale under-wing while the upper surface shows a similar dark area surrounded by buff-coloured feathers. It perches frequently on posts, fences, bushes and trees, its posture then looking more horizontal than that of other owls. Its food consists mainly of small mammals, principally field voles, and during 'plagues' of these animals the Short-eared Owl can be quite numerous.

Voice The song is a deep 'boo-boo-boo' uttered in circling song flight. It also has a barking alarm note, 'kowk', but is generally a silent bird.

Habitat Open country, moorland, marshes, heaths and dunes. In winter it frequents deserted airfields, margins of reservoirs, coastal marshes.

Nest A scrape well hidden in heather, grass or reeds. The 4 to 7 eggs are matt white, elliptical, and are laid late April or early May. It will raise two broods in vole-plague years.

Status A resident and winter visitor. Its preferred nesting habitat limits breeding distribution and consequently it is absent from the major part of the Midlands and S England. Also scarce in NW Scotland and absent from the Shetlands. Only two known instances of nesting in Ireland. Variations in breeding population occur according to food supply; in a poor year could be as low as 1,000 pairs.

Nightjar
Caprimulgus europaeus ♂

Characteristics 10½in (267mm). Over the centuries the twilight habits of this bird have given rise to many myths and legends. One old country name, Goatsucker, records the belief that at night it would suckle milk from goats. Other local names, such as Dor Hawk and Fern Owl, are more indicative of its activities. A strange bird in truth, resting up by day, eyes nearly closed, its cryptic coloration of grey-brown, mottled, spotted, streaked and barred with dark brown, renders it almost invisible against a background of earth and plant debris. The head is broad and flat with a very small bill, which opens to an enormous gape facilitating the capture of night-flying insects, particularly moths. Becoming active at dusk, it twists and wheels, flying with deliberate strokes interspersed with floating glides for which the wings are held in a deep V position. If seen quite close before the light goes, the white on the wings and tail of the male readily distinguishes the sexes. It perches lengthways on a branch, wall or building, resting on its breast, for its feet are small and not developed for gripping.

Voice It has a frequently uttered flight call 'coo-ic'. (Also during display it claps its wings over its back.) The song is a sustained vibrant churring sound, continuing on occasions for up to 5 minutes without a break. During this time a rhythmic rise and fall is apparent, as the bird turns its head from side to side. It does not sing until dark, continuing throughout most of the night. The song period is May until July, and less frequently in August and September.

Habitat Woodlands, commons, hillsides, moors and open areas with good cover of bracken, gorse or heather.

Nest On bare ground. The eggs, normally 2, are laid in late May or early June. Elongated and elliptical, they are off-white, marbled and spotted with grey, yellowish-brown and darker tints. Two broods are regular.

Status A summer visitor, arriving April to May, and leaving August to September. It has declined considerably in recent years and is now mainly concentrated in Southern England. A few nest in Ireland. Total population probably less than 5,000 pairs. A Schedule I bird.

(left) Female ; (right) male

and the encroaching dusk render them invisible, only their distant calls indicating their presence. On wet dull days they fly lower in their never-ending search for food, when large numbers feed over open stretches of water offering a good supply of insects. To see a concourse of these birds whirling and wheeling over the surface of a lake or reservoir is a remarkable sight, as they can slice the air at 60mph (96kmph). Their short legs and comparatively tiny feet (four forward-facing claws) only allow them to cling to rocks or masonry, and if grounded for some reason they cannot get airborne again. Swifts carry a parasitic louse fly and sometimes these can so weaken a bird that it is brought down.

Voice A harsh screaming call uttered by parties of birds in chasing flight.

Habitat Can be seen anywhere, but invariably the numbers are related to suitable breeding sites, chiefly buildings.

Nest Composed of material collected on the wing —grass, feathers, etc — cemented together with the birds' saliva, and usually sited under the eaves of houses or in a loft or other hole or crevice. Swifts will use specially constructed nest boxes. The 2 or 3 eggs are dull white, laid May to June. One brood.

Status A summer visitor, arriving late April or early May. The return passage begins in July and by the end of August most have gone, a few being still around in early September. Generally distributed throughout Britain and Ireland, it does not breed in NW Scotland, the Outer Hebrides, the Orkneys or the Shetlands. Total population probably around 100,000 pairs.

Swift
Apus apus

Characteristics 6½in (165mm). This most aerial of birds (it is reputed even to sleep on the wing) has a distinctive silhouette, with long, narrow scythe-like wings and a short tail. The sooty-brown plumage gives it a totally black appearance even at close range. On warm, clear, still summer evenings the crescent shapes of these birds can be seen spiralling upwards until height

Kingfisher
Alcedo atthis ♂

Characteristics 6½in (165mm). Quite a shy bird, surprisingly inconspicuous until it flies, it is perhaps not so well known in the wild as its brilliant plumage would suggest. In Victorian times, its appearance was widely appreciated, but as a specimen in a glass case more than as a living bird. In today's more enlightened times the taxidermist is not the cause of its reduction; pollution is now probably to blame. When perched, its tiny red feet and ruddy breast are more apparent, with long dagger-shaped beak and short tail giving the bird an oddly-proportioned look. The male's bill is totally black, and the female can be distinguished by a pale orange patch on the lower mandible. In flight the bird becomes a bright cobalt-blue dart, showing greenish reflections on head and wings. But one has little chance to appreciate its splendid colouring as it rapidly follows the course of a stream or canal, usually calling as it goes. It is an adept fisherman, securing fish with a sudden dive, not by stabbing but by grasping stickleback or bullhead, its usual prey, between the mandibles. The fish is beaten to death and swallowed head-first. In the absence of a perch it hovers before plunging into the water. It has been known to take dragonflies and other aquatic creatures.

Voice A shrill piping 'chee' or 'chi-kee'. The song, which is rarely heard, consists of a series of sweet trilling whistles.

Habitat Fresh water of all kinds: rivers, streams, canals, lakes, reservoirs. In the winter, tidal estuaries, drains and gutters of salt marshes.

Nest At the end of a 1ft to 3ft (½m to 1m) tunnel, usually in the earth bank of a slow-flowing stream, but sometimes quite a distance from the water. The eggs, 6 to 7, are white and laid on a litter of fish bones, April or May onwards. Two broods are raised, often from the same nest site. The nest hole can be recognised by a trail of evil-smelling slime which runs from the entrance.

Status A generally distributed resident where suitable habitat occurs, but rare or absent north into Scotland and unknown in the Hebrides, Orkneys and Shetlands. Local to scarce in western parts of Ireland. Population much affected by severe weather, and it suffered greatly in the winters of 1962-3 and 1978-9. The present population is probably less than 5,000 pairs. A Schedule I bird.

Green Woodpecker
Picus viridis ♀

Characteristics 12½in (318mm). The general habits of all woodpeckers are much the same. They ascend tree trunks in a succession of jerky hops, clinging to the bark with their zygodactyl feet (two toes forward and two toes backward) and supporting their inclined bodies with their stiff tail feathers. They will also move along the underside of a bough, but never descend head-first. The strong chisel-like bill is used in the search for insect food, but it is the long specially adapted tongue which allows the bird to extract insect larvae from deep holes and crevices. It also drums with its bill, making a far-carrying sound to proclaim its presence (though the Green Woodpecker rarely does). The Green Woodpecker is the largest woodpecker occurring in Britain, and is just as likely to be seen on the ground as in a tree, for it feeds extensively on ants. But whether seen digging up an anthill or in more typical woodpecker stance on a tree, its green plumage, darker above and paler below, with crimson crown, is distinctive. Additionally the face is black with a dark red moustachial streak bordered with black in the male, totally black in the female. The undulating flight is also characteristic and with the bright greenish-yellow rump is unmistakable. The juvenile resembles the adult but the head and under-parts are streaked and barred blackish.

Voice A loud ringing laughing note, typified by one of the bird's common names: Yaffle.

Habitat Open deciduous woodland or parkland with plenty of mature trees, heaths and open country with scattered trees, orchards, sometimes large gardens. Infrequent in coniferous settings.

Nest In a hole bored into a tree trunk, sometimes only 3ft (1m) or so from the ground, but usually much higher. The entrance has a distinctly rounded look as opposed to the following species. No nest material except a few wood chips. The 5 to 7 eggs are white, laid April to May. One brood.

Status A resident, generally distributed in England and Wales, the highest concentrations S and W of a line from the River Dee to the Wash. It has spread into Scotland in recent years but is still absent from northern areas and Scottish islands, the Orkneys and the Shetlands. Unknown in Ireland. Affected by severe weather, and following the 1979 winter the population may be down to 15,000 to 20,000 pairs.

R.A.H. 79

Great Spotted Woodpecker
Dendrocopos major ♂

Characteristics 9in (229mm). It is difficult to overlook this boldly patterned bird with its white shoulder patches, brilliant red under-tail coverts and red nape patch (absent in the female), for in addition to its distinctive appearance it is probably the noisiest of all our three woodpeckers, being responsible for most of the 'drumming'. This loud mechanical noise is produced by rapid hammering at a tree trunk or bough with the bill. This activity is most frequent from February to May, but is heard occasionally in other months. In addition to the usual diet of wood-boring insect larvae, it also takes nuts and seeds, often wedging cones, etc, into a crevice to help in extraction of fruit. Occasionally it takes nestling birds of other species, opening up the nest hole or nest box to get at them. It will visit gardens, taking suet and nuts.

Voice An abrupt far-carrying call, 'tchick, tchick', uttered at rest and in flight.

Habitat Woodland, orchards, parkland with mature timber, large gardens, and also agricultural land with plenty of hedgerow trees.

Nest In a hole bored into a tree trunk, usually 10-12ft (3-4m) above ground but often higher. Entrance noticeably elliptical. No nest material is used except a few wood chips. The 4 to 7 eggs are white and glossy, laid mid-May. One brood. The young are very noisy and come to the nest entrance when the parents return with food.

Status Resident, and well distributed in wooded areas. It has spread northwards in recent years, colonising coniferous woodland. Absent from the Orkneys, Shetlands, Hebrides and Ireland as a breeding bird. Total population estimated at 30,000 to 40,000 pairs.

113

flight might be seen, as it floats from tree to tree on fully spread wings. Its normal flight is of the usual undulating woodpecker type, but is slower and somewhat more hesitant. It is rarely if ever seen on the ground.

Voice A loud shrill 'pee-pee-pee-pee-pee' which could be confused with the Wryneck's call but lacks its musical resonance.

Habitat Woodland, well-timbered parkland, old orchards, large gardens, tall hedgerows with trees.

Nest In a hole bored into a tree, often on the underside of a sloping branch, usually at a considerable height but sometimes quite low down. It invariably excavates rotten wood and its small hole could be confused with that of the Willow Tit. Nest material is a few wood chips. The eggs, 4 to 6, are white and glossy, laid April to May. One brood.

Status A resident, scarce to locally common in parts of S England, but certainly our rarest woodpecker and virtually unknown from Lancashire northwards. Not found in Ireland. Total population probably between 5,000 and 10,000 pairs.

Similar or Allied Species The Wryneck (*Jynx torquilla*) has woodpecker-type habits, but its camouflaged pattern of grey and brown plumage, the upper-parts mottled, streaked and vermiculated like the Nightjar, and its barred under-parts, give it a totally different appearance from any woodpecker. Formerly much commoner, it is now a rare summer visitor, the few irregular breeding pairs being in SE England and a small area of Scotland. A Schedule I bird.

Lesser Spotted Woodpecker
Dendrocopos minor ♂

Characteristics 5¾in (146mm). This tiny woodpecker is often overlooked for it spends most of its time hunting for insect larvae high up in the topmost branches of trees, rarely descending to the lower trunk or larger branches frequented by the Great Spotted Woodpecker. When seen, however, its distinctive barred black and white plumage and small size immediately identify it. The male has a red crown, the female a white crown. Juvenile birds resemble adults but are brownish about the face, both sexes having some red on the head. The species also drums less frequently than *Dendrocopus major,* producing a much feebler sound — as one would expect from a less powerful bill. In spring its moth-like display

Lesser Spotted Woodpecker

114

Woodlark
Lullula arborea

Characteristics 6in (152mm). The differences between this bird and the Skylark are not immediately apparent and a close look is needed to detect the more strongly contrasting pattern of buffish-brown streaked with darker brown. The whitish eye-stripe meeting across the nape, the short tail with white tips, and a dark mark near the bend of the wing are features which help identify it. More than anything, however, it is the song and display flight which distinguish it from all others. Feeding on the ground in the manner of other larks it moves unobtrusively over the grass searching for insects, at times taking seeds. It perches freely in trees and bushes which the Skylark never does. Its flight is usually more undulating and jerky. It is also much less gregarious than *Alauda arvensis*, and is never seen in such numbers though it can be found in family parties after the breeding season.

Voice The call note is a melodious 'too-looeet'. The song is a sequence of short phrases comprising a few rich mellow notes interspersed with a liquid trilling 'lu-lu-lu-lu'. This is usually delivered at a constant height as the bird circles over a wide area, though also given from a tree or from the ground. The Woodlark frequently sings at night. It can be heard regularly from the beginning of March to mid June and occasionally at other times.

Habitat Heaths, commons, downlands with scattered trees and bushes, preferring light to dry soils. It also favours areas of recently felled woodland.

Nest A foundation of grass and moss, lined with finer grasses and some hair, situated on the ground partly hidden by low cover. The 3 to 4 eggs are whitish with variable brown freckling, less heavily marked than the Skylark's. Usually two broods.

Status A locally scarce resident. It has shown marked fluctuations, was formerly much more widespread, and is now confined to a few localities in Wales, East Anglia, SW and S England. Total population probably less than 500 pairs. A Schedule I bird.

Skylark
Alauda arvensis

Characteristics 7in (178mm). Famed for its song, the inspiration of poets, but to most people this bird is merely a black speck in the sky as it gives forth its unending stream of notes. At close quarters, its brown upper-parts are seen to be strongly streaked with black, the under-parts whitish with distinctive black marks on the breast. Like all larks it is a ground feeder, walking in a crouched position, but when alarmed it stands bolt upright with its crest raised. In the main its diet consists of seeds, worms and insects. Over short distances its normal flight has a rather fluttering wavering character, but when more prolonged its movement through the air is strong and slightly undulating. When it rises from the ground it shows conspicuous white outer tail feathers and noticeable whitish trailing edge to its wing. In winter it often occurs in quite large flocks. A charming collective term for such a gathering is an 'exaltation of larks'.

Voice The flight call is a clear rippling 'chirrup', and variants. The song is a loud continuous succession of warbling notes, delivered with great power as the bird rises on quivering wings, mounting higher and higher until almost lost to sight on occasions. It also sings while descending, dropping suddenly and silently, recovering a foot or so above the ground and then gliding a short distance before settling. It sings from posts and sometimes from the ground. The song is heard in most months of the year, most frequently in January to July.

Habitat Open country with short grassland preferred, but also any cultivated land, elevated moors, also marshes, coastal dunes, etc.

Nest A grass cup lined with finer grasses, on the ground, usually well hidden in grass or growing crops. The 3 to 5 eggs are dull white, heavily marked with dark and light brown spots and speckles, laid April to May. Two broods, sometimes three.

Status Present throughout the year. One of our commonest and most widely distributed birds, found virtually everywhere in Britain and Ireland with an estimated population of around 4 million pairs. Considerable immigration from the Continent during winter.

Sand Martin
Riparia riparia

Characteristics 4¾in (121mm). Smallest of the Hirundine family which includes the Swallow and House Martin, this bird is easily identified by its mouse-brown upper-parts and white underneath with a brown band across the breast. The tail is less forked and lacks the Swallow's long tail-streamers. The flight is also quite different, more fluttering and erratic than the graceful swooping movement of the Swallow. However, like the Swallow it is frequently seen hawking for flying insects over lakes, reservoirs or rivers, particularly during the first week or two of its arrival. Again like *Hirundo rustica*, it perches on telegraph wires and branches of bushes or other vegetation overhanging water. In autumn many congregate at communal roosts, usually in reed beds, when as many as 10,000 birds arriving at dusk make an impressive sight.

Voice A short 'chirrup' is the usual flight note, with a shortened alarm version. The song is a weak twittering like a continuation of its ordinary notes. Most frequently heard April to June.

Habitat Though the Sand Martin occurs in open country it is rarely found far from water or its nesting areas.

Nest A litter of grasses and feathers collected in flight are placed at the end of a 2-3ft (½-1m) long tunnel excavated in a vertical bank of earth or sand. Colonies are found in sand and gravel pits, on the banks of rivers, or cliffs, etc, and occasionally it uses drainpipes and holes in brickwork especially where this borders flowing water. The eggs, 4 to 5, are white and laid in May to June. Usually two broods.

Status A summer resident, often with first arrivals in early March, leaving in September with stragglers staying into October. A widespread nesting bird, but distribution is patchy, related to the availability of suitable nesting conditions. Scarce in N Scotland and absent from the Orkneys and Shetlands. It has declined generally in numbers since 1968-9, when the population crashed from around 1 million pairs to possibly only 250,000 pairs, believed to be the consequence of drought in its African winter quarters. Numbers are probably not much above this level today.

Swallow
Hirundo rustica

Characteristics 7½in (190mm). Regarded as the herald of spring more than any other migrant arrival; every birdwatcher's heart is surely gladdened by the sight of the first Swallow of the year as it dips low over the local lake or pond, hawking for flies, in early April. With its slender build, long wings, forked tail and long streamers it really cannot be confused with other members of the Hirundine family. The dark metallic-blue upper-parts, chestnut-red forehead and throat, and creamy-white under-parts should preclude confusion with either House Martin or Sand Martin. The Swallow has short legs but can perch quite easily, and also frequently settles on the ground to gather debris and mud for its nest. It hawks for food at a great height or on occasions barely skimming the ground, as determined by the altitude of the insects it seeks, which varies according to the prevailing atmospheric and seasonal conditions. Like the Sand Martin it is highly gregarious, and in autumn large numbers gather at communal roosts, usually in reed beds.

Voice The usual note on the wing is 'tswit-tswit-tswit', which when alarmed becomes 'twsee'. The song is a pleasant warbling twitter intermingled with short trills, uttered chiefly on the wing but also at rest. It is heard regularly from April until the middle of July, and occasionally until early September.

Habitat Open country, particularly cultivated land with farms, ponds, rivers and streams.

Nest A saucer-shaped construction of mud pellets cemented together by the birds' saliva, with some grass and straw woven in, lined with hair and feathers. It is usually fixed to rafters in a shed, barn or outhouse and often under a bridge. The 4 to 6 eggs are white and pointed, with dull red spots at the large end, laid May onwards. Two broods usual.

Status A summer visitor, arriving early April, leaving September to October with some stragglers into November. Found over almost the whole of Britain and Ireland but absent from some parts of Scotland. Total breeding population probably around ½ million pairs.

House Martin
Delichon urbica

Characteristics 5in (127mm). With its white under-parts, dark back and wings and white rump, this other member of the swallow family is readily identified as it swoops and flutters around buildings or over water. It frequently associates with both Swallows and Sand Martins, being no less a master of the air. In fact it regularly flies higher than the Swallow, often mixing with that high-altitude operator the Swift in pursuit of aerial insects, its basic food. Like the House Sparrow, this bird has developed an attachment to man, certainly where nesting is concerned, using buildings where once it would have sought out a cliff face; a few colonies are still to be found in such natural settings. It settles on the ground to collect mud for its nest, and its short, white, feathered legs are then conspicuous.

Voice The usual call is a distinct 'chirrup', with a shrill 'tseep' when alarmed. The song is a soft sweet twittering, less frequently uttered than the Swallow's, used from April to September.

Habitat Open country districts, including quite remote areas but more often around towns and villages.

Nest Made of small pellets of local mud, cemented together with the birds' saliva to form a distinctive inverted beehive-type construction. It is usually fixed under the eaves of a house or other building, frequently under bridge parapets. It is lined with feathers and other lightweight materials collected on the wing. The 4 to 5 eggs are glossy white and pointed, laid May onwards. Two broods, sometimes three. A colonial nester, with a few to several hundred birds at favoured sites. House Sparrows frequently take over old nests or even newly completed ones.

Status A summer visitor, arriving early April, leaving September to October, with a few stragglers of 1 around until early November. Generally di ibuted but more local than the Swallow. Absent from parts of N Scotland. Total British and Irish population around ½ million pairs.

R.A.H.

119

Tree Pipit
Anthus trivialis

Characteristics 6in (152mm). Most pipits are small brownish birds, streaked with dark markings, the various species identified by subtle differences in plumage and behaviour. They are in some ways similar to the larks, but usually much slimmer looking and more active. They even recall wagtails in their tail movements, though the tail is of course much shorter. This species and the Meadow Pipit are probably most likely to be confused with one another, but the generally sleeker appearance of the Tree Pipit should help distinguish it. The breast also tends to be a buffer colour with larger and generally fewer streaks. The legs are distinctly flesh-coloured and if seen really well the short hind-claw may be detected. The outer tail feathers are white, as in the Meadow Pipit.

Voice In flight utters a distinctive hoarse 'teez'. It also has a persistently repeated alarm note, 'sip'. The song has greater power than the Meadow Pipit's, ending in a number of shrill plaintive notes, 'see-er, see-er, see-er'. This is invariably delivered in a characteristic song flight from the top of a tree when the bird flutters upwards, begins to sing near the peak of its ascent and continues as it parachutes down, usually completing its sequence on return to the same or a nearby perch.

Habitat Open woodland, heathland, parkland, and grassland with scattered trees.

Nest Usually a depression on the ground, well hidden by vegetation but sometimes quite open. Built of dry grasses with a foundation of moss, lined with finer grass and some hair. The eggs, 4 to 6, show remarkable variety, ranging from pale blue to greenish, pinkish-brown or grey, sometimes freckled all over as those of other pipits, but can be blotched or spotted, laid in May. One, sometimes two, broods.

Status A summer visitor, arriving early April, leaving late July to October. A common breeding bird in parts of England and Wales, but scarce or absent from the East Midlands and East Anglia, becoming scarcer northwards into Scotland, particularly in the NE. Does not breed in Ireland, where it is a scarce passage migrant. Total British population probably around 10,000 pairs.

Meadow Pipit
Anthus pratensis

Characteristics 5¾in (146mm). A small brown streaky-looking bird, tending to be more lively and active than the Tree Pipit which it closely resembles. It perches less frequently in trees, but will use them freely when available. At close range a pale orbital ring round the eye is detectable and the orangish legs with a long rear claw are distinctive. During winter it occurs in loose flocks and when flushed rises from the ground in ones or twos rather than en masse, calling as it goes. In flight it rises and falls in a hesitant manner as if struggling to gain height, and when in the air the flocks never show the tight togetherness of other small birds on the move. It feeds mainly on insects, but worms, spiders, etc, and seeds, are occasionally taken.

Voice When flushed and in flight it has a weak 'peep-peep-peep' call. The song lacks the strength of the Tree Pipit's, but it has similar display flight, ascending from the ground with fluttering action, giving forth a sequence of tinkling notes, ending in a trill as it plummets earthwards. This can be heard regularly from April to July.

Habitat In the breeding season, elevated moorland particularly, but also rough grassland, heaths, sand dunes, salt marshes. In winter it moves to more lowland regions, sea coasts and the margins of inland waters.

Nest Built of dry grass and bents, lined with finer materials and some horsehair. Situated on the ground in a depression, often completely hidden by a tussock of grass or heather. The 4 to 5 eggs are off-white with a heavy speckling of brown or grey concentrated at the large end, laid at the end of April. Two broods. It is often host to a Cuckoo's egg.

Status Present throughout the year, with some immigration from the Continent during autumn. An abundant breeding bird in suitable areas but thinly spread or absent from English Midlands, East Anglia and parts of S England. Total British and Irish population probably over 3 million pairs.

Similar or Allied Species The Rock Pipit (*Anthus spinoletta*) is a larger, greyer-looking bird than either the Tree or the Meadow Pipit. It has dark legs and greyish, not white, outer tail feathers. Its call note is a distinctive 'fist'. Strictly a coastal bird, breeding all round Britain except E Coast from Flamborough Head round to the Isle of Wight, apart from a few localities on the South Coast. Also found all round Irish coast. Total breeding population around 50,000 pairs.

Meadow Pipit

Yellow Wagtail
Motacilla flava ♂♀

Characteristics 6½in (165mm). Wagtails are a confusing group of birds, with several species and a number of geographical races occurring in Europe. This, with their various states of plumage, makes specific identification difficult at times and impossible with some juveniles. Slim and graceful, wagtails spend much of their time on the ground, walking and running with a backwards-and-forwards motion of the head, the tail constantly moving up and down. They dart after small insects, frequently making a short fluttering flight to catch a passing fly. In summer plumage the male Yellow Wagtail is bright lemon-yellow on the face and under-parts, with the back yellowish-green and the tail black with white outer feathers. The female is duller-looking, browner on the upper-parts and paler underneath. Flight is strongly undulating, and when alighting the tail is elevated and spread. It perches freely on fences, posts, bushes and even trees at times. Outside the breeding season it is gregarious, and on migration can often be seen in groups of some numbers.

Voice The call is a loud musical 'tweep' uttered in flight or at rest. The song is a simple warble with call-notes mixed in, delivered in flight or when perched. Most frequently heard from May through to early July.

Habitat In the breeding season, damp marshy areas, rough pastures and cultivated fields usually with nearby water.

Nest Built of grass and rootlets lined with hair, wool and sometimes feathers. On the ground, usually well hidden by vegetation and frequently under a tussock or in a depression made by a horse or cattle hoof. The 5 to 6 eggs are pale buff with darker brown speckles and marbling, laid in May. More southerly nesting birds raise two broods.

Status A summer visitor arriving in early April, with main departure over by September, but some present until October. It has declined in recent years and is now mainly found from the Midlands northwards, becoming scarcer towards the Scottish border with a few scattered records beyond. A few nest in Wales, SW and S England. It formerly bred in Ireland but now only isolated occurrences of nesting. Total population around 25,000 pairs.

Similar or Allied Species The most likely identifiable race to be seen in Britain is the Blue-headed Wagtail *(Motacilla f. flava)*. The male has a blue head and white eye-stripe and chin. Blue-headed Wagtail and Yellow Wagtail sometimes interbreed.

R.A.H.

Yellow Wagtail

Grey Wagtail
Motacilla cinerea ♂

Characteristics 7in (178mm). In summer the male has a distinctive black patch on the throat, a white stripe above and below the eye, bright yellow under-parts and a grey back. The female lacks the black throat patch and is less yellow underneath. The species is considered by some to be the most graceful of our wagtails, and the longer tail with conspicuous white outer feathers certainly give it a more elegant appearance than either Pied or Yellow Wagtail. Its actions are very similar, feeding on insects found along stream sides where it also catches flies with a quick fluttering flight from boulder or stone. It frequently perches on tree branches overhanging water. Not so gregarious as other Wagtails, it is usually only seen in ones or twos.

Voice A distinctive metallic 'tizz-it' note, uttered in flight and at rest. The song is similar to the Pied Wagtail's, but more varied and musical. Infrequently given from early March to May, exceptionally at other times.

Habitat Prefers fast-flowing rocky upland streams for its nest, but also occurs along slower-running rivers and occasionally by reservoirs and other still waters which have sluices or overspills. In winter, it is more general along lowland streams, reservoirs and canals. It frequents city centres, feeding on pools of water which collect on flat roof-tops. Also found on the coast.

Nest Built of moss, dead grass, roots, lined with wool, hair and feathers. Sited on a ledge or a cavity in a bank, under a bridge or on a wall near running water. The 5 to 6 eggs are off-white, speckled or spotted with shades of grey, laid March or April onwards. Two or three broods.

Status Present throughout the year, common and widespread in Scotland, Wales and Ireland. Breeds sparingly in Eastern and Central England, and is absent or scarce in other localised areas lacking suitable nesting conditions. Total population 25,000 to 50,000 pairs.

Female

123

Pied Wagtail
Motacilla alba

Characteristics 7in (178mm). Probably the most familiar of the wagtails, this distinctive black and white bird with its long bobbing tail is met virtually anywhere, quite frequently in towns and cities feeding in parks or on flat rooftops. It walks with a brisk gait, head moving backwards and forwards and tail moving up and down as it searches for insects in the grass or rainwater puddles. It frequently makes sudden, fluttering leaps to chase small gnats and flies, a common feature of wagtail behaviour. The male has a black crown, throat and breast, blackish wings with two white wing bars, and a black tail with white outer feathers; the forehead, sides of the head and the belly are white. The female is generally paler-looking, being greyer on the back and less black on the head and breast. Juvenile birds have grey backs and dark face and breast markings, but otherwise are as their parents. In winter Pied Wagtails often roost together in large numbers in factory roofs and also in greenhouses and other buildings.

Voice The usual call is a shrill 'tissick' uttered on the ground and in flight. The song is a simple warbling twitter mainly heard in March and April, infrequently at other times.

Habitat This is a bird of most types of open country, particularly the vicinity of farms and other buildings; it also lives in cities and their suburbs, frequenting gardens and parks, playing fields and roadsides. In winter it is to be found particularly around the margins of inland lakes, reservoirs, streams, rivers and other watery places and on the coast.

Nest Built of moss, dead leaves, roots, etc, lined with hair, feathers and wool. Sited in holes and cavities in banks, behind ivy walls, buildings, etc, or open-fronted nest boxes. The 5 to 6 white eggs are speckled or spotted in shades of grey, laid April to May. Two broods, sometimes three.

Status A resident, generally and widely distributed throughout Britain and Ireland, but not breeding in the Shetlands. Total population around 500,000 pairs.

Similar or Allied Species The White Wagtail (*Motacilla a. alba*) replaces the Pied Wagtail on the Continent. It has a pale grey back and rump. A number occur in Britain on migration, being more readily identified in the spring.

(left) Pied Wagtail; (right) White Wagtail

Waxwing
Bombycilla garrulus ♂

Characteristics 7in (178mm). The prominent pinkish-chestnut crest of this starling-sized bird, along with its conspicuous yellow-tipped tail, white and yellow markings in the wing (except in the case of the female or first-winter males), black throat and eye-stripe, render it unmistakable. Normally, too, it is quite tame, allowing close approach, when it may be possible to see the strange oblong projections at the tips of the shafts of the secondaries (and very occasionally, also smaller ones on the tail feathers) which resemble lumps of red sealing-wax. These give this colourful and distinctive bird its name. The pointed wings and swift buoyant flight are starling-like, and except for its distinctive call the Waxwing could easily be mistaken for the commoner bird at a distance. A highly gregarious species, it invariably occurs in flocks, roaming the countryside feeding on berries. It can be seen perched in bushes, trees or tall hedgerows greedily devouring haws or rowan berries for which it will visit gardens

Voice A high trilling 'sirrrrr'.

Habitat Anywhere with suitable berry-bearing trees or shrubs, and is as likely to be found along a hawthorn-bordered country lane as in a sub-urban garden.

Status A winter visitor, with a few being noted in most years. Periodically, when 'irruptions' take place, large numbers visit these shores, arriving along the eastern coast and generally spreading westwards, sometimes reaching Ireland — depending on the extent of the invasion. The last major irruption occurred in 1965-6.

Dipper
Cinclus cinclus

Characteristics 7in (178mm). Looking something like a large Wren, this sturdy rotund bird is unique for its underwater feeding behaviour. It walks or plunges into water, walking on the bottom to seek out caddis fly or mayfly larvae and other aquatic insect life. It also feeds on small molluscs, crustacea, fish, tadpoles and worms. On the surface, it can swim buoyantly. When perched on a stone or boulder in the middle of a fast-flowing stream even its silhouette is distinctive, especially as it bobs and curtsies as if on hinged legs. From close range it can be seen that the white gorget is bordered below by a chestnut band merging into the black belly. The head and nape are chocolate brown, the rest of the upper-parts a slaty black with a scaly look. The eye appears to flash white as the bird rapidly opens and closes its upper eyelid: the nictitating membrane is transparent and is closed when the bird is under water. Flight is direct and rapid, usually low down, following the course of a stream; the bird often indicates its approach by its call notes. Young birds have grey upper-parts and are much whiter underneath than the adults.

Voice A loud 'zit-zit-zit'. The song of both sexes is a sweet rippling, rapid warble, usually delivered from a branch overhanging water. It sings in most months.

Habitat Swift upland streams in moorland and hilly areas, the margins of lakes and tarns in mountainous country. To a lesser extent it is also found in more lowland regions where streams and rivers are slower-moving. In winter it moves down to larger rivers and sometimes estuaries and the seashore.

Nest A big domed affair, like a large Wren's nest but with the entrance more over-hung. The dome and foundations are moss, the grass cup interior lined with leaves. Invariably situated over fast-moving water, under a ledge or under the exposed roots of a waterside tree, frequently under bridges and behind waterfalls. The eggs, usually 5, are white, laid end of March onwards. Two broods, sometimes three.

Status Present throughout the year, the Dipper is confined to hillier regions of Britain, being totally absent from England east of a line from the Humber south to the Isle of Wight. It does not breed in the Orkneys, Shetlands, Isle of Man and southern tip of Cornwall. Generally distributed in Ireland but absent from some central parts. Total population probably around 30,000 pairs.

Wren

Troglodytes troglodytes

Characteristics 3¾in (95mm). This tiny brown bird with its powerful voice is amongst the best known of all garden birds. Its distinctive little round shape with cocked tail identifies it immediately, even in silhouette. It perches briefly on a fence or branch before flying with a quick whirring action of its short stubby wings to some other position. When hunting for food, which is usually low down or on the ground, it is so small and mouse-like that it is soon lost to sight, disappearing behind the scantiest of vegetation. It probes every nook and cranny for insects and spiders with its fine bill, never still for a minute. At night it roosts in holes and crevices, also in nest boxes; in winter a dozen or more will huddle together in one box.

Voice A strident prolonged mixture of notes delivered with explosive force, usually terminating in a high trill. It sings at virtually any time throughout the year. It also has a harsh 'chit-chit' note which becomes a churring noise when alarmed.

Habitat Woodland, gardens, anywhere with good cover, often in reed beds in winter.

Nest A number are built, believed entirely by the male, and are left half-finished or unlined. These are called 'cock' nests. The completed nest is made mostly of dead leaves with a lining of moss, hair and feathers. It is usually in a crevice or hole, or in ivy and creepers on walls, frequently in the roots of upturned trees. It can be in odd situations such as in an old jacket hanging in a garden shed or in the crease of a folded newspaper caught in a wire-strand fence. The 5 to 6 eggs are white with reddish-brown freckles, usually at the large end, and are laid in April. Two broods.

Status A resident, perhaps our commonest nesting bird, found throughout Britain and Ireland. Population now about 10 million pairs. It suffers high mortality in long periods of freezing weather.

Dunnock
Prunella modularis

Characteristics 5¾in (146mm). An unobtrusive little bird with a brown, well-streaked back, grey head and breast. It is easily overlooked as it creeps about hedgerow bottoms with short jerky hops searching out small insects, spiders, etc, which form the major part of its diet, with seed added in winter. Though commonly known as the Hedge Sparrow, with its fine insectivorous bill it is certainly no sparrow, and does in fact belong to the Accentor family. Often on the ground but as likely to be seen perched on a bush or fence giving a quick burst of song, for it is a regular garden visitor. Its characteristic wing-flicking gives it another common name, Shuffle Wing. A solitary species.

Voice A frequently uttered shrill piping 'tseep' which is more prolonged when given as an alarm note. The song is a not unmusical hurried jingle of notes, shorter in duration and less powerful than the Wren's. Can be heard during most of the year but less often in the autumn.

Habitat Hedgerows, spinneys, copses, scrubby bushy areas, gardens, almost anywhere where suitable cover exists, even penetrating city centres.

Nest A neatly constructed cup of moss and hair on a foundation of moss, twigs, roots and leaves. Frequently in a hedge or bramble, usually low down and well hidden, but a wide variety of sites used. The 4 to 5 eggs are deep blue and rather pointed, laid April to May. Two or three broods. A frequent host for a Cuckoo's egg.

Status Present all the year, breeding widely throughout Britain and Ireland, only absent from the more mountainous regions of Central Scotland and Shetland. Sparse in the Hebrides. One of our commonest birds, having an estimated British and Irish population of 5,000,000 pairs.

Robin
Erithacus rubecula

Characteristics 5½in (140mm). Many birds are more brightly coloured and may even be better songsters, but of all British birds the Robin is our best loved. It has appeared on our postage stamps, is annually featured on millions of Christmas cards and was voted our National Bird. A regular garden visitor it can become tame enough to take food from the hand and quite often stays to nest. When the young leave the nest they are spotted all over, lacking the orange-red breast of the adult, though their typical Robin behaviour and perky stance is immediately recognisable. From August to mid-winter it is strongly territorial and aggressively drives off its own kind, as well as other species, from whichever area it chooses as its own. It normally feeds out in the open, hunting small insects and spiders. Some seed, fruit and berries are also taken and it will do almost anything for meal-worms. On the Continent it is a bird of deep woodland, where it is shy and retiring. The sexes are indistinguishable.

Voice A persistent scolding 'tic-tic', particularly uttered prior to roosting. The song is a short mixture of warbling notes, with a melancholy quality, which can be heard at most times of the year. The female also sings.

Habitat Gardens, hedgerows and woodlands with plenty of undergrowth.

Nest Built of moss, rootlets and dry grass, lined with hair, commonly situated in a hollow or recess in a bank, or amongst ivy, or frequently in discarded tins, utensils, etc; the Robin will also use open-fronted nest boxes. The 5 to 7 eggs are whitish with light red freckles, usually at the large end, laid March to April. Two broods, sometimes three.

Status Present throughout the year, it is one of our most widely distributed birds though perhaps scarcer in parts of N Scotland and the Hebrides. Total British and Irish population around 5,000,000 pairs.

129

Nightingale
Luscinia megarhynchos

Characteristics 6½in (165mm). Widely known for its song rather than its appearance, due to the male's habit of singing at night when other birds are silent. Poets have certainly found plenty of inspiration from this: Keats, Coleridge, Arnold, Munro and many others have extolled its powers, and indeed few people remain insensitive to its rich melodic phrasing. To see the bird is a different matter, for it is a shy, skulking creature, keeping to cover, generally quite low down, taking only short quick flights; then the rufous upper-tail coverts and tail are conspicuous. Otherwise it is uniform brown on the upper-parts with pale greyish under-parts, tending to be whitish on the throat and abdomen. When viewed in the open its kinship to the Robin is evident, with the tail frequently cocked. Juvenile birds have a spotted and mottled appearance, looking much like young Robins. It feeds on the ground, taking worms, insects and spiders; fruit and berries are also eaten.

Voice A soft 'wheet' call, similar to Chiff-chaff and Willow Warbler, also a hard 'tacc-tacc' or softer 'tucc-tucc'. The alarm call is a harsh 'kerr'. The song is a loud and rich succession of repetitive phrases, often commencing with a bubbling 'chooc-chooc-chooc-chooc' followed by a flutey 'piooo' repeated slowly, rising to a magnificent crescendo. Usually this is delivered from low cover, but on occasions it sings from an exposed perch. It can be heard regularly from mid-April to early June, then infrequently for the rest of the month and exceptionally in July. Though best known for night singing it also sings during daytime.

Habitat Open deciduous woodland having plenty of low cover, with a preference for damp moist places. Large old gardens, thickets, bushy places, tangled hedgerows are also favoured.

Nest Consists mainly of dead leaves, lined with dead grass and often some hair. Can be on the ground, well hidden in woodland litter or under low brambles, but sometimes is off the ground in a tangle of brambles. The 4 to 5 eggs are olive green, laid in May. One brood.

Status A summer visitor, arriving mid-April, leaving August. Breeds locally, not extending much beyond a line N from the Humber to the Severn, apart from a number found to the N of Shrewsbury. Does not breed in Ireland. Has declined since the 1950s, probably due to habitat loss. Total population about 10,000 pairs.

Black Redstart

Phoenicurus ochruros ♀

Characteristics 5½in (140mm). This delightful little bird has the typical fiery Redstart tail which quivers markedly when it perches, but its darker colouring and lack of orange on the under-parts readily distinguish it from the commoner species. The head, throat and breast of the male are black with a noticeable white patch on the wing. The female, however, is nondescript, though always looking darker than the female Common Redstart. The juvenile is also very similar, but at all ages the orange-red tail is apparent. Some young males breed in immature plumage, looking more like females with little or no white in the wing. Behaviour and action are similar to the Redstart's, but its habitat preference is usually sufficient to distinguish the species. Adept at hawking for insects on the wing, hovering as it does so, it more frequently feeds on the ground, taking a variety of small beetles and flies, and berries in autumn and winter.

Voice The call note is a brief 'tsip', often followed by a scolding 'tuc-tuc' alarm. The song is a short warble, finishing with a noise like a bag of ball-bearings being shaken together. Heard from March to July, also August to early October.

Habitat In the breeding season this is a bird of urban areas, particularly near old derelict buildings with nearby waste ground. Also on industrial sites, near gasworks, power stations, etc. In winter, open waste places are frequented.

Nest Built of grass, moss and fibres, lined with hair and feathers, it is situated in a cavity or on a ledge, or perhaps on rafters under eaves, etc. The 4 to 5 eggs are glossy white with small red-brown spots, laid April onwards. Two broods.

Status The Black Redstart has colonised Britain in recent times. It bred on a derelict site at Wembley in 1926, and there followed a number of scattered records from other parts of London. During World War II the many bombed sites encouraged more pairs to nest. Other urban areas and some coastal cliffs have been colonised, with numbers fluctuating widely. London and the SE of England are still the centre of population, with other scattered records from E Anglia and the Midlands. Average breeding total only 30 pairs. A Schedule I bird.

Male

male's fine colours but has the same distinctive tail. Young birds out of the nest are rather like young Robins but also have the characteristic tail colouring. An active bird, flitting constantly amongst the branches, often making short fluttering flights after insects, it also feeds on spiders, small worms and sometimes berries. As the Black Redstart, it shows an affinity to the Robin, having the same general carriage and bobbing action.

Voice Usually an urgent 'whee-tic-tic' but it also has a plaintive 'wheet' note similar to Willow Warbler or Chiff-chaff. The song is a brief hurried jingle trailing away to a mixture of curious mechanical-sounding notes.

Habitat In the breeding season, old deciduous woodland and parkland, heaths and commons with scattered trees; also open hilly country with stone walls.

Nest Usually in a hole in a tree or stump. Frequently uses nest boxes, also holes in buildings or a wall, sometimes ledges in the open. Material used includes grass, bark, moss and roots, lined with hair and feathers. The 5 to 7 eggs are pale blue, sometimes with small red-brown spots, laid May onwards. Often two broods.

Status A summer visitor, arriving mid-April, return passage starting in July and lasting until October. Locally found in suitable areas throughout Britain, being scarcer in E and S England. Sparse in NE Scotland, absent from the Hebrides, the Orkneys and the Shetlands. Sporadic nesting records from Ireland. Total population between 50,000 and 100,000 pairs.

Redstart
Phoenicurus phoenicurus ♂

Characteristics 5½in (140mm). The adult male is an extremely colourful bird, having a black throat and face with a white forehead, blue-grey upper-parts and orangey-red under-parts, the same as the rump and tail. It is this orangey-red tail which the bird vibrates frequently with a rapid up-and-down movement, that often draws attention to its presence. The female lacks the

Female

Whinchat

Saxicola rubetra ♂

Characteristics 5in (127mm). Chats are small colourful birds of open country, perching freely on the tops of bushes, stems and stalks, with this species and the Stonechat likely to be confused with one another, certainly at a distance. However, when seen well, the male Whinchat's striking head pattern of browns and black with a bold white eye-stripe is distinctive. The back has a rich pattern of black and brown, the under-parts are a warm buff. In flight there are broad wing marks which are most evident, while the sides to the base of the tail are also noticeably white, contrasting with a black terminal band. The female has these features, but they are all less pronounced except the tail pattern. The 'Furze-chat' as it is sometimes called perches on a topmost spray attracting attention with its repetitive alarm call until with low jerky flight it moves to another vantage point, which might be a telegraph wire, tree top or stone wall. Its diet is mainly insects and it tends to feed more actively at dusk. In autumn small groups can be seen together on passage.

Voice A scolding 'tic-tic, tu-tic, tic'. The song is a brief variable warble, not distinct from that of other chats but usually richer and more Robin-like.

Habitat In the breeding season, open country ranging from bracken-covered hillsides and upland pastures to lowland meadows, commons and marshy areas. On migration can be found in a variety of situations such as coastal dunes and similar open places.

Nest A dry grass and moss foundation lined with fine bents, rootlets, often hair, wool and feathers. Usually well hidden in grass or dead bracken. The 5 to 6 eggs, deep greenish-blue with fine red speckles near large end, are laid May onwards. Two broods.

Status A summer resident, arriving late April with return passage from July through to October. Formerly more widespread in S and E England, now only found locally in these areas. In Britain it is basically a bird of upland areas, mostly in Wales, the North and West. Sparse in Eastern Scotland and not breeding in the Shetlands. The bulk of the Irish population concentrated in the central lowlands with virtually none in the S and NE. Total British and Irish population 20,000 to 40,000 pairs.

Male

Stonechat

Saxicola torquata ♀

Characteristics 5in (127mm). Resembles the Whinchat, but is a plumper, more upright bird, perching on the tops of bushes, constantly flirting its tail and flicking its wings. In summer plumage the male's head is black with white patches on the sides of the neck; there is also a white wing patch and a whitish area on the rump. The under-parts are orange-chestnut and the tail is dark. The female is a drabber version of the male and lacks the white rump and neck patch. In autumn and winter the male's markings too are less distinct, with juvenile birds looking similar to the female. The Stonechat mainly feeds on the ground, darting from its perch to take an insect, caterpillar or spider, but it will frequently capture moths and flies on the wing. Seeds are occasionally eaten. In flight the white in the wing is noticeable, while the bird's shorter-tailed, rounder-winged look should rule out the Whinchat.

Voice A harsh 'wee-tack, tack' like the sound of two pebbles struck together — hence the name. The song is a short mixture of sweetish notes, a bit like a Dunnock at times, delivered from a perch or in a dancing display flight, most frequently from March to June.

Habitat In the breeding season, gorsey, brambly areas, commons, hillsides, uncultivated country with rough grassland and scattered bushes, particularly near the coast. In winter it frequents the above but also wanders to inland areas where it does not breed, and is frequently found on derelict industrial sites.

Nest Built of grass, moss, bracken, heather and gorse, etc, lined with fine grass, hair, wool and feathers. Frequently in a gorse bush, but often deeply hidden in grass or bracken. The 5 to 6 eggs are pale blue with red-brown speckles near the large end, laid March to April. Usually two broods.

Status A resident, but has declined considerably in recent years and is now a sparse breeding bird inland, mainly confined to western coastal regions. Widespread in Ireland but locally scarce or absent in the SE and NE. Total British and Irish population probably around 50,000 pairs.

Male

Wheatear
Oenanthe oenanthe ♂

Characteristics 5¾in (146mm). One of our earliest summer migrants to arrive. It is always a delight to see the first returning birds (males arrive before the females), with their pearl-grey upper-parts, broad white stripe over the eye, black ear coverts and wings, and buffish under-parts. It is, however, the distinctive white rump which usually catches the eye as the bird flies with swift jerky flight. The females, which turn up a week or two later, are brown above and buff below, with the blacks replaced by dark brown; they too have the white rump. Active and restless they are constantly on the move, hopping along the ground, flitting from stone to stone or clump to clump, bowing and bobbing and moving the tail up and down. The body is held erect and the bird always looks alert as it perches on stone walls, fences, wires and sometimes bushes — rarely in trees and then in the topmost branches, not among foliage. During migration it is often seen in small parties.

Voice A hard 'chack-chack-weet-chack-chack-chack'. The song is a short pleasant warble which includes some Skylark-type notes, delivered from some prominence and sometimes in flight, mainly from April to mid-June.

Habitat In the breeding season, moorland, hilly country, upland pastures, heaths, downs and coastal dunes. On migration, can occur anywhere and is often seen on airfields, golf courses, playing fields, wasteland, etc.

Nest Built of grass, roots, moss, lined with fur, hair, wool and feathers. Located in a cavity or recess, such as rabbit burrow or hole in a stone wall, under boulders, etc. The 5 to 6 eggs, pale blue, sometimes with small red spots, are laid late April to May. Usually one brood.

Status A summer visitor, arriving early March, leaving August to September, with stragglers into October and sometimes November. Has declined as a breeding bird in this century and is now very sparse on Southern downlands. Generally scarce and found locally W of a line from the Humber to the Severn. In Ireland mainly concentrated towards the western half of the country. Population of Britain and Ireland probably around 80,000 pairs.

Similar or Allied Species The Greenland Wheatear (*Oenanthe o. oenanthe*) is a larger, more brightly coloured subspecies, occurring on migration; it can then be identified, particularly in spring, not normally arriving before May. It perches in trees more frequently than the Wheatear.

Wheatear

135

Ring Ousel
Turdus torquatus ♂

Characteristics 9½in (241mm). The Mountain Blackbird, as it is sometimes called, is unlikely to be seen away from areas offering suitable habitat, except in migration when it can turn up anywhere — though not so frequently met with on passage as are some other migrants. In most respects looks like a Blackbird, but the male can be identified by the white crescent on the breast. The secondaries and coverts have greyish edges so that the closed wing appears pale grey, a feature also evident when it flies. Partial albinism is common among Blackbirds and sometimes birds with some white plumage might resemble a Ring Ousel; this possibility should be borne in mind when a 'Ring Ousel' turns up in the garden! The female has a less distinct gorget, but has the pale grey area in the wing. Juveniles lack the gorget and look like young Blackbirds. Food and feeding behaviour are similar to those of the Blackbird.

Voice The alarm call is similar to the Blackbird's but distinctly harsher. The song is loud and clear, lacking the Blackbird's fluty variety and more akin to the limited repertoire of the Mistle Thrush. Most frequently heard from late March to mid-June.

Habitat In breeding season, mountains and moorland, hillsides with bushes and trees.

Nest Built of coarse grasses with heather and twigs, and earth in the foundation, lined with finer grasses. Situated on a heather-covered bank or on a rocky crag or gully, sometimes in a bush or small tree, and occasionally on stone buildings or walls. The 4 to 5 eggs are like well-marked Blackbird's eggs, laid April to May. Usually two broods.

Status A summer migrant, arriving March-April leaving September-October. Found in elevated areas of SW England, Wales, N England and Scotland where suitable habitat occurs. Has declined in numbers in recent years, particularly in Ireland where few now nest. Population of Britain and Ireland probably 8,000 to 16,000 pairs.

Male

Blackbird
Turdus merula ♂

Characteristics 10in (254mm). One of our most familiar birds, the male Blackbird with his glossy black plumage, orange-yellow bill and yellow eye-ring, is unmistakable. The female, on the other hand, is dark brown with a whitish throat; the young birds out of the nest look like the female but are gingery-brown on the head and breast. As a frequent garden visitor it provides ample opportunity to observe its behaviour, which is generally more skulking than that of other thrushes. Though it eats berries of all sorts from hedgerow or bush, it is basically a ground feeder, turning over dead leaves and other litter to get at spiders and insects. It also takes worms and small molluscs, etc. In flight it appears weak and hesitant, usually only travelling short distances. On alighting the tail is raised in a slow graceful way and the wings frequently drooped. Generally a shy, nervous bird, it is easily frightened, flying off giving a noisy alarm call. It is a frequent road casualty as it swoops low when flying from one side to the other.

Voice A low 'tchook-tchook', and when startled it has a characteristic rattle. Before going to roost it utters a persistent 'pink-pink-pink', often a number of birds chorusing this together. Described as one of our finest singers, its song has a rich fluty quality, lower-pitched, richer and mellower than that of the Song Thrush, usually finishing with a few weak creaky notes. The song period begins in December, but not until February is the full song regularly heard, continuing until July and ceasing entirely in August.

Habitat Most types of countryside, particularly woodland, hedges, gardens, commons, also hillsides with scattered bushes, almost overlapping with the Ring Ousel in some areas. It has even penetrated into towns and cities.

Nest A rather bulky affair, a foundation of moss and grasses with a mud cup further lined with finer grasses. Usually positioned a few feet from the ground in hedge or bush, but frequently in banks, garden sheds or against fences; it will use ledges provided for the purpose. The 3 to 5 eggs are greenish-blue with underlying grey marks freckled with reddish-brown, often zoned at the large end. Two and frequently three broods, and the same nest will be used.

Status Mainly resident, but considerable immigration in late autumn, with birds leaving February-April. Has increased and spread a great deal in recent times and is now probably one of our most abundant birds with a British and Irish population of 7 million pairs.

Female

Fieldfare
Turdus pilaris

Characteristics 10in (254mm). This almost Mistle Thrush-sized bird is particularly a feature of the winter countryside, when it can be seen in large flocks, foraging in the fields for worms, spiders and insect food or feeding on hedgerow berries, especially hawthorn. It is usually quite shy and not easily approached, but when viewed at close quarters it is readily distinguished by its pale grey head and rump, chestnut-brown back and tail. The crown is streaked black, the whitish flanks are boldly marked with black. In flight, the white under-wing is conspicuous as in the Mistle Thrush, but the latter is rarely seen in such large numbers and the call is different. Juveniles are much like adults but the greys are browner.

Voice A noisy bird, keeping up a constant chattering. The flight call is a harsh 'chack-chack-chack-chack'. The song is a rapidly uttered mixture of squeaky notes usually to be heard from April to June.

Habitat In the breeding season, this is diverse including woodland edges, moorland valleys, farmland, forestry plantations. In winter it ranges far and wide in search of food, particularly favouring open country. In really hard weather some come into gardens and feed on rotten fruit.

Nest Similar to the Blackbird's, reinforced with mud below the grass lining. The eggs, 5 to 6, are also much like those of the Blackbird, laid in May. Sometimes a second brood.

Status Mainly a winter visitor, arriving August to September, departing early March to May. In recent years has nested, the first known occurrence being in the Orkneys in June 1967. In subsequent years it has nested annually on Shetland and at several localities on the Scottish mainland. Also a few scattered occurrences in N England, as far south as Staffordshire, probably no more than 20 pairs nesting in any year. A Schedule I bird.

Song Thrush
Turdus philomelos

Characteristics 9in (229mm). No less familiar than the Blackbird, a regular garden visitor often to be seen on the lawns with head cocked on one side as if listening — it is in fact looking for signs of food. If nothing is to be found at a particular spot it will run forward with a few quick steps, stop and look again. It soon locates a worm and then a tug-of-war commences, the bird rocking back on its feet to wrest it from the soil. At other times it hops quickly on its flesh-coloured legs, for it seldom walks. A generally warm-brown bird on the upper-parts, it is yellowish-buff underneath with small dark brown arrow-headed marks rather than round spots. It is much more genteel than its congener the Mistle Thrush, invariably coming off second-best in any territorial dispute with other species. As well as eating worms, insects and spiders, it is partial to snails, hammering the shell on a regular 'anvil', a particular stone or hard piece of ground.

Voice The flight call is a soft 'sip', shorter than the Redwing note. The alarm call is a short harsh rattle. As much a songster as the Blackbird, its delivery is louder and clearer, being a succession of simple phrases of considerable variety, repeated over and over again, followed by a short pause before continuing. Often to be heard in December and in the early part of the year then most frequently from February through to July and sometimes in August.

Habitat Woods, thickets, hedgerows and gardens.

Nest Built of grass and roots and at times moss, leaves and twigs, with a smooth earth cup reinforced with small pieces of rotten wood. Usually situated in hedge or bush, early nests are often in quite exposed settings. The 4 to 5 eggs are blue, sparsely speckled and blotched with black, laid March to April onwards. Two or three broods, sometimes reared in same nest.

Status Present throughout the year, with some movement of resident birds and an immigration of Continental birds in winter. As widespread as the Blackbird (but absent from the Shetlands) though less numerous, with the total British and Irish population around 1 million pairs.

Redwing
Turdus iliacus

Characteristics 8¼in (210mm). Smallest of our commonest thrushes, it superficially resembles the Song Thrush, but can be immediately distinguished by the broad creamy stripe over the eye and the rich chestnut-red beneath the wings. Most widely known as a winter visitor it roams the countryside in flocks, often in the company of Fieldfares, foraging in the fields for worms and insects. In hard weather it resorts more to the hedgerows, feeding on berries, particularly yew holly and ivy. In really severe conditions of prolonged ice and snow it will come into gardens and towns. It is a nocturnal migrant, and arriving birds can be detected by their distinctive flight call, heard as they pass unseen overhead.

Voice The call is a thin 'see-eep' uttered in flight. The song is a series of descending fluty notes (usually 5), audible at quite a distance. A muted warbling sub-song can be heard from individuals among flocks on sunny days in February and March.

Habitat In breeding season, the edges of woods, wooded hillsides, shrubberies with lawns and tall trees. Outside breeding season, the open country, grasslands and hedgerows.

Nest Built of grass, twigs, moss and wool with a thin mud cup with an inner lining of fine grass. Often situated low down in the fork of a tree or in a bush. The eggs, 5 to 6, are like small Blackbirds', laid in May to June. Two broods.

Status Mainly a winter visitor arriving in September or October, leaving March or April. Some nest. The first record of nesting in Scotland was in Sutherland in 1925, with intermittent breeding over the next 41 years, but from 1967 the number of birds breeding in N Scotland has increased; the population was around 300 pairs, but is now probably much lower. A Schedule I bird.

140

Mistle Thrush
Turdus viscivorus

Characteristics 10½in (267mm). Though usually shy and not very approachable it is an aggressive bird in competition for food, and fearless in defence of its nest and young, driving off much larger birds and even attacking humans on occasions. It spends much of the time on the ground, when its upright stance and more assertive look are apparent. It is a much greyer bird than the smaller Song Thrush and more boldly marked with bigger broader spots. The sexes are similar. In flight it has a striking white underwing and white-tipped outer tail feathers, a feature not shared with any other thrush. Its mode of flight is also distinctive, with prolonged closure of its wings at regular intervals, and when descending to land it makes several gliding swoops following on from each other before finally settling. Though it takes worms, spiders and insects its food is largely fruit and berries, with a fondness for ivy, yew and hawthorn. Despite its name it does not eat mistletoe!

Voice A harsh churring note, uttered in flight and at rest, becoming louder and more rattling when alarmed. The song is a limited number of loud notes, Blackbird-like but less fluty, repeated again and again. Usually delivered from the top of a high tree, often in rain and high wind, giving rise to its common name, Stormcock. Most frequently heard from early February until June.

Habitat In the breeding season, farmland, woodlands, gardens, orchards, parkland and sometimes open, almost treeless country.

Outside the breeding season, it frequents rough pasture, arable land and wild open hilly country.

Nest Built of moss, grasses, roots, strengthened with earth and lined with fine grasses. Bits of wool, feathers and other items often woven in give a most untidy look. It is built, typically, in the fork of a tree, 10-12ft (3-4m) above the ground. The eggs, 3 to 5, creamy-buff or greenish-blue with red-brown spots and blotched, are laid March to April. Frequently two broods, sometimes using the same nest.

Status Present throughout the year, with some immigration from the Continent during winter. A widespread bird, breeding throughout Britain and Ireland but scarce in some areas of N Scotland and the Hebrides, and absent from the Orkneys and the Shetlands. Total British and Irish population between 300,000 and 600,000 pairs.

141

Grasshopper Warbler
Locustella naevia

Characteristics 5in (127mm). This secretive skulking warbler would frequently go undetected but for its peculiar mechanical song, as most of its time is spent low down in the undergrowth, often on the ground, where it scuttles about almost mouse-like, searching for insects, spiders and the like. It normally sings from an exposed perch, though rarely at any great height. When located (which can be difficult as the song is far-carrying), careful approach should allow a close enough view to see its olive-brown coloration, darkly streaked back and buffish under-parts. The rounded tail is a distinctive feature and when flushed from the undergrowth this and the oval-shaped wings should aid identification.

Voice The call note is a hard sharp 'tchick'. The song is a rapid high-pitched trill often lasting for up to 2 minutes. It also has a ventriloquial effect, sounding near, then far off, due to the bird moving its head from side to side. It frequently sings at dusk and at night. Mainly heard from late April to the end of July, occasionally in August and September.

Habitat Open areas with thick low cover, bushes, brambles, also heathland, downland and marshy areas with tangled vegetation.

Nest Built almost entirely of dead grass with a finer grass lining and sometimes some hair. Well hidden on or near the ground. The eggs, 5 to 6, are pinkish, often tinged purplish-grey, usually marked with find red-brown speckles, laid in late May to early June. Usually two broods.

Status A summer visitor, arriving late April to May, leaving August to September. Widely but locally distributed, being mainly absent from upland areas. Total British and Irish population around 25,000 pairs, but possibly much higher.

Sedge Warbler
Acrocephalus schoenobaenus

Characteristics 5in (127mm). Commonest of our waterside-haunting warblers, and more widespread than the Reed Warbler, from which it is easily distinguished by a prominent creamy stripe over the eye, even when only a brief glimpse is obtained. A closer more protracted view can often be obtained as the bird sings from a reed stem or bush; this will reveal its brown, boldly streaked crown and upper-parts, shading to yellowish-buff on the flanks. Chiefly an insect-eater, it creeps about in thick cover, seldom coming out into the open for long, though it makes frequent short quick flights; the plain rufous rump can then be seen. It also has a long conspicuous song flight, rising into the air then parachuting down, singing all the time.

Voice A sharp 'tucc' often repeated, and when the bird is excited this becomes a scolding rattle. It also has a grating 'churr' note. The song is a mixture of musical and harsh chattering notes, more varied than that of the Reed Warbler. It includes long trills and mimics other birds; sometimes sings at night.

Habitat Though mainly found in damp places, marshy areas, osier and reed beds, the Sedge Warbler is frequently found in somewhat drier conditions, such as overgrown ditches and thick hedgerows with tangled vegetation.

Nest A rather solidly built affair, with a foundation of moss and grasses and a lining of finer materials including feathers and hair. Usually located low down in thick vegetation, it is sometimes in a bush. The 5 to 6 eggs are pale, covered with dense yellow-brown markings, usually with black hairlines. Laid May-June. One, sometimes two, broods.

Status A summer visitor, arriving mid-April, returning August-September. Generally distributed over most of England where suitable habitat exists, being rarer in the SW, the North, Wales and N Scotland, absent from the Shetlands. Common in Ireland, breeding widely. Total population of Britain and Ireland around 300,000 pairs.

Similar or Allied Species The Aquatic Warbler *(Acrocephalus paludicola)* is a similar-looking bird, but has a broad buff band down the centre of the crown. Some young Sedge Warblers have a distinct pale streak on the crown, but never as pronounced as the Aquatic Warbler's. A rare visitor. The Cetti's Warbler *(Cettia cetti)* is not necessarily a reed-hunting species, but likes damp areas with tangled undergrowth, where its skulking habits make viewing difficult. Looks not unlike the Nightingale, but smaller and the tail less rufous. Song is a sudden explosive burst of notes rather like the warbling part of the Nightingale song. Has begun to nest in SE England in recent years. A Schedule I bird.

Sedge Warbler

143

Voice The usual note is a low 'churr'. The song is in some way like the Sedge Warbler's, but slower and more conversational, with a 'twangy' character. Sometimes it sings on the wing and not infrequently at night. It is heard regularly from late April to mid-July, occasionally in August and early September.

Habitat Reed beds and waterside vegetation.

Nest A unique construction of grass and reeds lined with finer materials, including feathers, wool and hair, woven round and supported by several reed stems. Always about 3ft (1m) above water, it has a deep cup for the 3 to 5 eggs, which are greenish-white marked with dark olive-brown and grey blotches. Laid May-June. Two broods in S England.

Status A summer visitor, arriving late April, leaving August-September. A colonial nester, it is to be found locally where suitable habitat exists. Mainly S England, East Anglia, the Midlands, Cheshire and S Yorkshire. Rare in Scotland and Ireland. Population 400,000 to 800,000 pairs.

Similar or Allied Species The Marsh Warbler (*Acrocephalus palustris*) is a very similar-looking bird, best identified by its completely different and beautiful song. This is remarkable for its diversity and amazing mimicry. It also breeds in a different situation, building a 'basket-handle' slung nest. It is a rare summer visitor, confined mainly to the Severn and Avon valleys. A Schedule I bird. Savi's Warbler (*Locustella luscinioides*) superficially resembles a large Reed Warbler but has a Grasshopper Warbler-type song. A few pairs nest in S and E England, and it appears to be increasing. A Schedule I bird.

Reed Warbler
Acrocephalus scirpaceus

Characteristics 5in (127mm). Plain brown above and whitish below, this bird has no striking features. But even if the inexperienced observer is unable to identify it straightaway, it cannot be confused with the Sedge Warbler as it has hardly any eye-stripe and also lacks the streaky head and back of the other bird. Though not shy, it rarely leaves its reedy world, where it spends the day in chattering song or feeding on aquatic insects. However, with a little patience it can usually be seen, as it hops from stem to stem or pushes its way through the tangled vegetation. At other times it can be seen sidling up to the top of a reed to sing in full view.

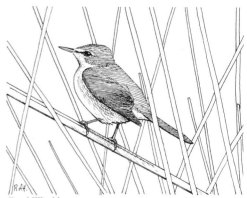

Reed Warbler

Dartford Warbler
Sylvia undata

Characteristics 5in (127mm). This dark-looking bird is very skulking and, on wet windy days particularly, is not inclined to show itself, keeping low down in thick undergrowth, making satisfactory observation very difficult. In fine weather it is more likely to perch freely on top of a bush or spray of vegetation, and can be seen to have a slate-grey head (with crown feathers frequently raised) shading to dark brown upper-parts. The under-parts are dark purplish-brown with the chin and throat spotted with white. At really close range a ruby-red eye and crimson eye-ring are discernible. The long tail is regularly cocked and frequently flicked. If flushed the bird will only fly a short distance, close to the ground in a weak erratic way, the tail bobbing up and down as it goes. In autumn small groups gather and wander about together. It feeds chiefly on insects.

Voice A grating metallic 'tchirr', and a short 'tuc' becoming a rapidly uttered 'tutututututucc' when excited. The song is a short Whitethroat-like warble, most frequently heard from March to July.

Habitat Open commons and heathland with heather and gorse.

Nest Built of dead grass, sometimes incorporating heather, dead gorse, moss, etc, with a lining of down, hair, rootlets and occasional feathers. Situated low down in the heather or gorse. The 4 off-white eggs are finely spotted with brown and grey, laid April to May. Two broods.

Status A resident in fluctuating numbers, being extremely vulnerable to severe weather. After virtual extinction following the winter of 1962-3 it has increased to around 560 pairs. At present it is confined to an area from Devon to Sussex, with the vast majority located in Dorset and Hampshire. A Schedule I bird.

Whitethroat
Sylvia communis ♂

Characteristics 5½in (140mm). A skulking bird at times, it does however normally proclaim its presence from the top of a bush or hedgerow with regular bursts of lively song. Always active and alert, it will deliver a few notes from one vantage point, then slip into the shelter of the foliage to reappear somewhere else with another snatch of song. It usually allows the observer a sufficiently good view to see that the male has a pale grey cap extending to the nape and below the eye, a pure white throat, rufous-brown wings contrasting with a dull brown back and a pale pinkish breast. The female is duller, with a brownish head and only a trace of pink on the breast. Young birds are almost entirely rufous-brown. Flight is usually short, with jerky flits from bush to bush, when the longish tail with white outer tail feathers is obvious. Food is mainly insects but in autumn also berries and soft fruits.

Voice A scolding 'charr' and a repeated 'tack-tack', also a subdued 'wheet-wheet, wit-wit-wit'. The song is a scratchy jumble of notes of short duration, often delivered in display flight, when the bird rapidly ascends, singing as it goes, then suddenly drops back to cover. Heard most frequently from mid-April to July.

Habitat Open country, rough ground with bushes and tangled vegetation, commons, untrimmed hedgerows and edges of woodland.

Nest Quite a substantial structure of dry grass with a deep cup lined with black hair, usually low down in a bush or brambles. The 4 to 5 eggs are pale greenish or stone coloured, with markings ranging from big blotches to fine stippling, laid May onwards. Usually two broods.

Status A summer visitor, arriving mid-April, departing July onwards, with late birds still around in early October. In Britain and Ireland it is generally distributed, but is sparse and local in N Scotland, the Hebrides, the Orkneys and Shetlands. A commoner bird before 1969, when barely 25 per cent of the previous year's birds returned from winter quarters in West Africa, where prolonged drought is believed to have caused many deaths. Some recovery has been made since, but the present population of about 500,000 pairs is still well below the 1968 peak.

Female

Lesser Whitethroat
Sylvia curruca

Characteristics 5¼in (133mm). More secretive than the previous species, and does not show itself so freely, singing from the depths of some hedgerow or bush rather than in the open; its distinctive notes are often the first indication of its presence. When seen well, its most prominent features may be a pair of very dark ear coverts on the grey head contrasting with the white throat, creating a masked appearance. The female's face pattern is less distinct but there may be difficulty in separating the sexes. The Lesser Whitethroat also lacks the warm brown of the wings and the whiter outer tail feathers of the Whitethroat, though its flight and general behaviour are much the same. The diet is mainly insects, but in autumn also fruit and berries.

Voice The call notes, 'chikikikikikik', resemble the Whitethroat's, but the song is completely different, being a succession of loud notes a little like the Yellowhammer's. This 'rattle' is often, though not always, preceded by a soft low musical warbling, only audible at close range. Song period is from late April to the end of June, less frequently heard in July and exceptionally later on.

Habitat Similar to the Whitethroat's, with a tendency to favour taller, thicker hedgerows, larger gardens and shrubberies.

Nest Smaller than the Whitethroat's, lacking its thick base, but comprised mainly of stalks and roots, sometimes only lined with roots but often with horsehair. The 4 to 6 eggs are creamy-white, rather sparsely blotched with dark-centred yellowish spots and underlying grey, laid May onwards. Sometimes two broods.

Status A summer visitor, arriving April, departing August to September. Generally distributed throughout England, but local and scarce in the SW and also N of the Humber, becoming increasingly rare; totally absent in Scotland, scarce or absent from most of Wales and entirely absent from Ireland. Total breeding population between 25,000 and 50,000 pairs.

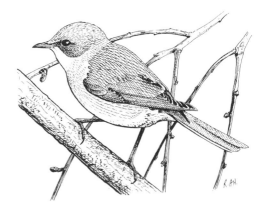

Garden Warbler
Sylvia borin

Characteristics 5¼in (133mm). A uniform brownish warbler with pale under-parts and no distinguishing features to proclaim its identity.

However, with experience, its plumper look, round head, stubby bill and short tail are points to note, though the song alone should prevent confusion with other species. An active yet secretive bird, it moves quietly about the foliage feeding on insects, sometimes taking spiders and worms, and in autumn fruit and berries.

Voice The 'chak-chak' call note is softer than the Blackcap's, and it also has a low grating 'churr'. The song is a continuous rapidly uttered mellow warble somewhat like the Blackcap's but often of longer duration and lacking the sudden crescendo. It is usually delivered from cover, often while the bird is moving about, and heard regularly from late April to mid-July.

Habitat Open deciduous and mixed woodland, with plenty of undergrowth, also thickets and areas of overgrown hedges.

Nest Built of dry grass and stems with occasional leaves and bits of moss, lined with fine grass, small roots and some hair. Situated low down in tangles of brambles, also in briars, gorse or other thick vegetation. An untidier nest than the Blackcap's or Lesser Whitethroat's. The 4 to 5 eggs are similar to the Blackcap's, but usually glossier-looking, laid May to June. One brood, occasionally two.

Status A summer visitor, arriving mid-April, returning August to September. More locally distributed in England than the Blackcap, being scarce or absent from the Fens, W Cornwall and SW Lancashire. Sparse in Scottish lowlands and found in only scattered localities of N Scotland. Occurs in only a few areas of Ireland. Total British and Irish population 60,000 to 100,000 pairs.

Blackcap
Sylvia atricapilla ♂

Characteristics 5½in (140mm). Unlike the Garden Warbler, this bird is immediately recognicable on sight, the male having a sharply defined black cap extending to the level of the eye, while the female has a less conspicuous though equally distinctive reddish-brown cap. Additionally, this species is greyer-looking than other similar-sized woodland warblers, being greyish-brown on the back and paler underneath, the legs black. Not a showy bird and generally keeping to cover; as most other small warblers it is not keen to make protracted flights, much preferring to use foliage to hide its whereabouts. But it is less retiring than the Garden Warbler. During the summer its food is mainly insects, but in the autumn and winter it takes fruit and berries. It also visits bird tables, feeding on such items as cake and bread.

Voice The call is a sharp 'tack-tack' like two pebbles struck together; it also has a churring alarm note. Its song is a mixture of low warbles rising to rich melodic notes, more distinct than the Garden Warbler's though the phrases are much shorter. The quality of its song is considered to be on a par with the Blackbird's and Nightingale's and it is sometimes referred to as the Northern Nightingale. Mainly heard from April to the end of June, and occasionally as late as September.

Habitat In the breeding season, open woodland, copses and spinneys with dense undergrowth, and other overgrown places with trees.

Nest A neat structure of dry stems and grasses, lined with finer material and sometimes horsehair. Usually situated in a bush or hedgerow, amongst honeysuckle or briars, etc. The 4 to 5 eggs are light brown, blotched and marbled with darker brown, laid May onwards. Sometimes two broods.

Status A summer visitor, mainly arriving early April, leaving August to October. An increasing number overwinter each year. Fairly well distributed in England and Wales, becoming increasingly local and scattered northwards into Scotland. Scarce in Ireland. Total population estimated at 200,000 pairs.

Male and (foreground) female

Wood Warbler
Phylloscopus sibilatrix

Characteristics 5in (127mm). Largest and most brightly coloured of our leaf warblers, this strictly arboreal bird is quickly identified by its contrasting yellowish-green upper-parts, sulphur-yellow throat and breast and white belly. There is also a broad yellow stripe above the eye. Its behaviour is similar to the Chiff-chaff's and Willow Warbler's, but it does not flick its tail. The wings, however, are longer, evident during its butterfly display flight as the male spirals down to settle by the female. When seeking its food it frequently makes short dashing flights after insects, or hovers to pick them from leaves. In the autumn berries are sometimes eaten.

Voice Has two distinct songs. For one, the bird utters a few preliminary notes, running into a shivering trill delivered with head up, wings and tail vibrating; the other is a single note, 'puu', repeated about a dozen times. This second song is often introduced at intervals in the sequence of number-one song. Alarm call is a plaintive 'puu'.

Habitat Beech and oak woodlands, particularly with some sloping ground, not necessarily with much undergrowth.

Nest A domed construction of grass, dead bracken and dead leaves, lined with finer grass and occasionally some hair. Situated in a natural hollow in the ground, invariably on a slope, often with little surrounding cover. The 5 to 7 eggs are white, thickly speckled with purplish-brown and some grey underlying marks, laid May to early June. One brood.

Status A summer visitor, arriving mid-April, leaving August, with stragglers into September. Some decrease in recent years, probably due to habitat loss, but still widely distributed where suitable nesting areas occur. Locally scarce in the English Midlands and absent from parts of E England, parts of Scotland, the Hebrides, the Orkneys and Shetlands. Extremely scarce in Ireland with only a few breeding records. Estimated population around 30,000 to 60,000 pairs.

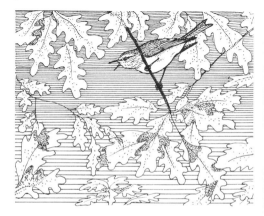

Chiff-chaff
Phylloscopus collybita

Characteristics 4¼in (108mm). This species and the Willow Warbler are slim graceful active little warblers, very similar in appearance but having distinctive songs. Generally duller-looking, the Chiff-chaff has browner upper-parts and more buffish under-parts than the Willow Warbler. The legs are usually dark but this is not always a safe identifying feature. First arrivals in spring are often to be seen low down in hedgerows searching for insect food, but later in the season they tend to feed higher up in tree cover, flitting from branch to branch catching flies with a quick dash or hovering to pick insects from a leaf. The restless activity is heightened by the regular flicking of the wings and tail.

Voice The usual call is a soft plaintive 'whweet' much like a Willow Warbler's. The song, however, is the unmistakable repetition of single notes of varying pitch, which gives the bird its name, uttered in an irregular sequence, sometimes without a break for 15 seconds or longer, usually delivered from well up in a tree and often while moving about in branches. It is regularly heard from March onwards to mid-July, and again less frequently until early October, with migrating birds singing on passage.

Habitat In the breeding season, woodland with plenty of undergrowth. Seldom found in conifers.

Nest An untidy domed construction of leaves with an interior of grass stalks and moss and a lining of feathers; normally situated off the ground in brambles or creepers, etc. The eggs, usually 6, are white, evenly spotted with purplish-brown, laid May onwards. Usually two broods.

Status A summer visitor, mainly arriving in early March, returning from August through to October. Most years a number overwinter in S England, S Wales and SW Ireland. As a breeding bird it is well distributed in England and Wales, but scarcer northwards, being sparse or absent in NW Scotland, the Orkneys and Shetlands. Well distributed in Ireland. Total British and Irish population estimated at 300,000 pairs.

Willow Warbler
Phylloscopus trochilus

Characteristics 4¼in (108mm). Easily confused with the Chiff-chaff, except in song. It often feeds quietly amongst the foliage, when subtle differences of plumage such as the rather more greenish-looking upper-parts and the yellower under-parts, with the legs usually appearing a palish brown, are important. Flight and behaviour are almost identical to the Chiff-chaff's, but it is perhaps less restless, though it flicks its wings just as much. It also feeds in the same manner, occasionally fly-catching and hovering to pick insects from under leaves, but it is less tied to tree cover and is often found well away from woodland. Young birds are even yellower looking than the parents.

Voice The call is similar to that of the Chiff-chaff but more of a 'hoo-eet'. The song is a beautiful silvery cadence and has been described as 'a tender delicious warble with a dying fall, mounting up round and full then running down the scale to expire upon the air in a gentle murmur'. It is heard regularly from early April until early July, and again with same frequency in early August.

Habitat Open woodlands, bushy commons, and almost any place where considerable ground cover plus a few trees exists.

Nest Domed, of mosses, grass or bracken, and invariably lined with feathers; usually on the ground, among grass in a hedge bottom, bank or open space in woodland, occasionally low down in a bush. The 6 to 7 pale eggs have fine red speckling, but may be heavily blotched, laid May onwards. Sometimes two broods.

Status A summer visitor, arriving early April, departing July to September with stragglers into October. Occasionally recorded in winter. Our commonest and most widespread warbler, there are few areas in Britain and Ireland where it does not nest. Absent only from the Fens, but sparse in the Hebrides and Orkneys, with sporadic breeding in the Shetlands. British and Irish population could well exceed 3 million pairs.

Goldcrest
Regulus regulus   ♀

Characteristics 3½in (89mm). This bird and the Firecrest are Europe's smallest birds. They are as restless and agile as warblers and tits, in whose company the Goldcrest is often found in autumn. Absurdly tame at times, on other occasions the Goldcrest is exceedingly difficult to locate, feeding high up in the tops of trees with only its calls to indicate its presence. When seen close to, the dull greenish upper-parts and flanks, whitish-buff under-parts and two white bars with a broad black band in the wings are noticeable features. However it is the coloured crest, bordered with black, which is distinctive, being orange in the male and lemon-yellow in the female. The young bird lacks this and might be mistaken for the rare Yellow-browed Warbler (*Phylloscopus inornatus*), though the small size alone should discourage this confusion. Food is chiefly spiders and insects.

Voice A frequently uttered high-pitched 'zee-zee-zee'. The song is also a thin high-pitched note, repeated rapidly about half a dozen times with a little terminal flourish; heard from March to July. The frequency range of the bird's voice renders it inaudible to some birdwatchers.

Habitat In the breeding season, coniferous and mixed woodland. At other times it also occurs in thickets, copses, along hedgerows, etc.

Nest A hammock of moss and spiders' webs, freely lined with feathers. Slung from a branch, usually towards the extremity, it is often only a few feet (a mere metre or so) from the ground, at other times quite high up. The 7-8 eggs are buffish-white with fine brown markings at one end, laid April onwards. Two broods.

Status Present throughout the year. Some southward movement in autumn with immigration from the Continent. As a breeding bird, the Goldcrest is generally distributed, but more local in the Midlands and parts of N England, absent from the Fens, scarcer in NW Scotland and the Scottish Highlands. Exceedingly common in Ireland. The increase in afforestation has undoubtedly benefited the Goldcrest, but it is susceptible to cold weather and was much reduced in the winter of 1962-3. Its population in Britain and Ireland was estimated at 1½ million before the hard winter of 1978-9.

Similiar or Allied Species The Firecrest (*Regulus ignicapillus*) is a similar-sized bird, but readily distinguished by a conspicuous white stripe above the eye and a black stripe through it. The whole plumage is brighter than the Goldcrest's. A much rarer bird, it has bred in recent years in a few localities in S England. A Schedule I bird.

(above) Goldcrest; (below) Firecrest

Spotted Flycatcher
Muscicapa striata

Characteristics 5½in (140mm). An inconspicuous mouse-brown bird (the sexes are similar), and not really spotted at all, having only a few dark streaks on the upper part of its whitish breast. The young fledglings, however, have a distinctly spotted look, far more deserving their name. If the adult bird's appearance is undistinguished, its pose and behaviour readily identify it. It sits in a very upright position on a branch or post, flicking its wings and tail, making frequent short aerial sallies after insects, often returning to the same perch. The flight is then fluttering and erratic, twisting and turning in the pursuit of its prey, which rarely if ever escapes. It requires open space for its manoeuvres, so its lookout post is usually found on the outskirts of woods, in woodland clearings or perhaps in a farmyard where a building serves as a vantage point. Generally a solitary bird, at immigration times it may be found travelling in loose association with others.

Voice A shrill 'tsit' and a 'tsee-tucc' alarm call. The song is thin and squeaky, a few quickly uttered notes rendered something like 'sip-sip, see, sitti-see-see'. It is most frequently heard from May to July.

Habitat Open woodland, parks and gardens.

Nest A loose affair of moss, wool, hair and cobwebs lined with roots, hair and some feathers, typically sited on a small ledge or cavity in a wall, behind ivy, on top of a post or beam or in the fork of a tree. The 4 or 5 eggs are greenish or blue-grey with rich chestnut spots and streaks, laid late May to early June. Usually one brood.

Status A summer visitor, not normally present before May, returning August to September with occasionally stragglers staying to October. Generally distributed throughout Britain and Ireland, it is rare in N Scotland and only breeds spasmodically in the Orkneys and Shetlands. The breeding population of Britain and Ireland is probably between 100,000 and 200,000 pairs.

Pied Flycatcher
Ficedula hypoleuca ♂

Characteristics 5in (127mm). The male in breeding plumage is a conspicuous black and white bird, the female more soberly attired — brown above, whitish below, with some white in wings and tail. Possibly less adept at flycatching than the Spotted Flycatcher, it seldom if ever returns to the same perch after chasing an insect, and in fact spends much of its time taking caterpillars from foliage. It also frequently feeds on the ground. On settling, particularly, the wings are flicked and the tail is moved up and down. Juveniles have a scaly-patterned plumage, similar to the Spotted Flycatcher, but show white in wings and tail much as adults. After the young fledge, the adults move up into the tree canopy and moult into autumn plumage in which both look like the female.

Voice It has several frequently used notes including a metallic 'whit' and an anxious 'phweet'. The song is a short simple phrase rendered 'tzit, tzit, trui, trui'. It is seldom heard after June.

Habitat Deciduous woodland, particularly oak and birch, in hilly country with rivers, streams or other water.

Nest Loosely built of bark, moss and roots, lined with hair and sometimes wool or feathers. It is usually located in a hole or cavity in a tree or building, and the bird readily takes to nest boxes. The 5 to 8 pale blue eggs are laid in May. One brood, exceptionally two.

Status A summer visitor, arriving late April and leaving in August or September. It has a generally westerly distribution, being common in most of Wales, the Lake District and parts of SW England. It breeds in scattered localities in Scotland, but has never nested in Ireland. The total population is probably around 20,000 pairs.

Female

155

Bearded Tit
Panurus biarmicus ♂

Characteristics 6½in (165mm). The male is a most handsome bird with a lavender-grey head and striking black 'moustaches'. The back and long tail are tawny coloured, the under-parts pinkish. The under-tail coverts are black and the tiny bill is yellow, which colourful combination should prevent confusion with any other species. The female is not so distinctive, lacking the grey on the head, the moustaches and the black under the tail, but in any case the bird's behaviour and habitat preference should be sufficient to identify it. It eats insects and seeds, the latter particularly in winter. These are usually obtained low down in vegetation with only the birds' call betraying their presence. They move up and down the reeds with a jerky action, assuming a variety of acrobatic tit-like postures. When at the top of a reed stem the Bearded Tit frequently takes a short flight with rapid whirring wing action accompanied by a peculiar rhythmical movement of the tail. It is very disinclined to fly in windy weather. Young birds resemble females but have a blackish middle of the back and sides of the tail, sometimes with dark streaks on the head. In autumn parties of birds rise into the air circling and calling excitedly. This is often the prelude to a migratory movement or irruption which occurs after a number of successful breeding seasons.

Voice A metallic 'ping-ping'.

Habitat Confined exclusively to reed beds in breeding season. After irruptions can occur in other vegetation around watery places.

Nest Dead reed leaves and sedges with a lining of flowering reed tops and occasionally some feathers. Eggs, 5 to 7, are white with streaks, spots and scrawls of grey-brown, laid mid-April onwards. Two broods, sometimes three.

Status A resident, with some immigration from the Continent. Formerly it bred over most of E England, but loss of habitat, and persecution by collectors and trappers, led to drastic reduction in numbers. Also it is seriously affected by severe weather. Still mainly confined to Norfolk, Suffolk and Leighton Moss in Lancashire, it has recently established itself in several other areas along the S coast as far west as Radipole in Dorset, but the total breeding population is probably less than 500 pairs. A Schedule I bird.

(left) Female; (right) male

Long-tailed Tit
Aegithalos caudatus

Characteristics 5½in (140mm). As its name suggests, this delightful little pink and black bird is nearly all tail, only 2½in (64mm) of its length being body. In winter little bands of these birds can be seen roaming the countryside, feeding along the hedgerows or in woods. Restless and active, flicking their wings and tail, they behave in much the same way as other members of the tit family, investigating every branch and twig as they search for small insects; seeds and buds are also occasionally eaten. As they move through the branches they call frequently to one another in order to maintain contact, for the flock keeps strung out, rarely bunched together. In flight the Long-tailed Tit looks top-heavy as with rapidly whirring wings it crosses open spaces. Over longer distances, its irregular undulating movement and long tail give it a most characteristic appearance.

Voice A low abrupt 'tupp' and a trilling 'tsirrup' are the usual calls, and it also has a 'zee-zee-zee' note, similar to other titmice calls but more penetrating. The song is little more than a mixture of calls, and is uttered infrequently.

Habitat Dense hedgerows, thickets, edges of woods, overgrown bushy areas. An infrequent garden visitor, it rarely lands on bird tables.

Nest The remarkable domed nest of moss, cobwebs and hair is beautifully decorated with grey lichens and lined with many feathers. The entrance is usually in the side, near the top. It is built in a bush, often gorse or thorn but many other types are used; it may be in a hedgerow and is quite often in the fork of a tree. The 7 to 12 eggs are white with very fine reddish speckles, laid late April. One brood. When the bird is sitting it can be seen near the nest hole, its tail folded over its back, protuding over the top of its head.

Status A resident, widely distributed, but scarce in some areas where the habitat is unsuitable, particularly in exposed treeless areas of N England and Scotland. It is susceptible to severe weather and its numbers were much reduced in the 1962-3 winter. Its population in Britain and Ireland is probably around 150,000 pairs.

Similar or Allied Species There is a northern race of Long-tailed Tit which has a pure white head but otherwise is similar to the British race. It is rare in Britain.

Marsh Tit
Parus palustris

Characteristics 4½in (114mm). This bird's name is misleading, for though it does occur in damp places it has no fondness for marshes and is more frequently found in woodland or hedgerows, searching the foliage for insects, preferring the lower growth to the upper canopy. It performs with the same agility as other tits, frequently hanging upside-down, often on one leg. The Marsh Tit and Willow Tit are very similar, but generally the Marsh Tit's black cap appears glossy and not so extensive on a smaller, rounder-looking head. Though some birds show a pale area in the wing this feature is more usual in the Willow Tit, but in order to be certain of identification its call needs to be heard or its nesting behaviour observed. A sedentary species, staying very much in its own territory and not apparently taking part in the irruptions typical of some other titmice.

Voice A distinctive double 'pitchuu', often preceded or followed by a 'tchair, tchair, tchair'. The song is a simple repetition of notes, with a liquid bubbling quality, regularly heard mid-January to mid-April, exceptionally at other times.

Habitat Deciduous woods, especially open oak woods, copses, hedgerows, orchards and occasionally gardens.

Nest In a hole or cavity in a tree or fence post, or perhaps in a wall, with a cup of hair, fur and down. Will readily take to nest boxes. The 6 to 8 eggs are white, lightly spotted with red-brown, laid April to May. One brood.

Status A resident, generally distributed in Wales and the southern half of England, scarcer northwards, absent from Scotland and Ireland. Population between 70,000 and 140,000 pairs.

Willow Tit
Parus montanus

Characteristics 4½in (114mm). Only since the beginning of this century has this species been definitely separated from the Marsh Tit, which it closely resembles. No single difference (apart from the call) is truly diagnostic, and the problem of distinguishing between the two still defeats many birdwatchers. On the whole the best plumage distinction is considered to be the light patch on the secondaries in the closed wing, though in summer this tends to be less obvious due to abrasion of the feathers, and some Marsh Tits too show a pale area in the wing on occasions. The sooty-black crown tends to be more extensive and is also a useful pointer, while the looser texture of these feathers suggests a slightly ragged appearance. The young of both Marsh and Willow Tit have sooty-brown caps and are virtually impossible to tell apart. Food is as the Marsh Tit's. Also a sedentary species, not known to move any great distance from its established territory.

Voice A buzzing 'eez-eez-eez' call with other high-pitched notes and a loud 'chay' are among the most frequently uttered sounds. However, a prolonged emphatic 'zi-zurr-zi-zurr, zurr' is absolutely diagnostic and may be heard at any time of the year. Song is infrequent and unlike other tit utterances, comprising a series of rich warbling notes most often heard from January to May and from July to September.

Habitat Similar to the Marsh Tit's, but more frequently found in damp woods and marshy places where soft rotten tree stumps are to be found. In winter it roams the countryside, frequenting hedgerows, thickets and overgrown areas; an uncommon garden visitor.

Nest In a cavity excavated by the bird itself in a soft rotten stump, usually birch, willow, elder or alder. Material used for lining is moss, grass, wood fibre and a few feathers. The 6 to 9 eggs are white with variable brown markings, laid from April to May. One brood.

Status A resident in England and Wales. Locally scarce in many areas, absent from parts of SW England, N Wales, the Fens, NW England and much of Scotland. Not known in Ireland. Total breeding population between 50,000 and 100,000 pairs.

Crested Tit
Parus cristatus

Characteristics 4½in (114mm). The acrobatic behaviour of this little bird resembles that of other tits, though when seen well there is little likelihood of confusion, aside from its rarity: for the black and white crest (duller in immature birds) and black and white face pattern is distinctive. The brown upper-parts and whitish under-parts complete the picture of a most attractive species. It feeds on insects and larvae, often searching for them in Treecreeper-style. Pine seeds and berries are also eaten. It regularly comes to bird tables in areas where the species occurs. In spring it can be located by its courtship display, when it circles tree tops calling as it goes. It is less sociable than other tits, and to see more than one together is unusual.

Voice A distinctive spluttering trill, unlike any other tit. The song is somewhat similar to a Blue Tit's.

Habitat Pine forest, particularly with dead and decaying wood; also found in mixed woodland.

Nest In a hole excavated in an old decayed pine stump, occasionally in elder or birch, sometimes in fence posts. Material used is mainly moss, with a lining of hair, feathers and wool. The 5 to 7 eggs are white with dark red spots, laid April to May. One brood.

Status The most restricted British breeding tit, confined to the Scottish Highlands. There is some evidence of a spread and increase in numbers within the last decade, though the total population does not exceed 1,000 pairs. A Schedule I bird.

Coal Tit
Parus ater

Characteristics 4¼in (108mm). Smallest of the tit family, probably even more active and restless than all the other members of this acrobatic group of birds. It is certainly more gregarious, often occurring in quite sizeable flocks in areas where it is common. A black-capped, white-faced bird, it differs from the Great Tit not only in size, but in its greyer, duller-looking upper-parts and buff under-parts. The major distinguishing feature is, however, the large white patch on the nape which is easily seen as it seeks out insects from the foliage and branches with its fine slender bill. Seeds are sometimes eaten, and, like other tits, it will feed on nuts, meat and fat at bird tables. Another useful identifying mark is a double, white wing bar, also quite visible in flight.

Voice A plaintive piping 'tsu', also a thin 'tsee-tsee-tsee'. The song is a repeated double note 'see-too, see-too', usually delivered high up in a tree, mostly from January to June and less frequently at other times.

Habitat Woods and copses with a marked preference for conifers. In winter, woodlands, hedgerows and gardens.

Nest Comprises moss and hair, fur and feathers. Situated in a hole or cavity in a tree, or at times in a hole in the ground. Freely uses nest boxes. The 8 to 11 eggs are white with fine red-brown speckles, laid April to May. One or sometimes two broods.

Status A resident, generally distributed, having increased in recent years, probably due to afforestation, though locally scarce in the Fens, Wales and parts of NW Ireland. Virtually unknown in the Orkneys, Shetlands and Hebrides. Total British and Irish population about 1 million pairs.

Blue Tit
Parus caeruleus ♂

Characteristics 4½in (114mm). With its bright blue crown, white face and generally yellowish-green upper-parts, the Tom Tit — as it is affectionately called — is a regular visitor to the garden, where its acrobatic performances at the bird table are a delight to behold, especially when peanuts suspended in a bag or dispenser are provided. In spring a pair of these engaging birds might be seen investigating every nook, cranny and hole in their effort to find a suitable nest site, calling to each other as they do so. In winter foraging bands of Blue and other titmice, sometimes also other small birds such as Goldcrests and Treecreepers, move through woodland or along a hedgerow in loose association, in a never-ceasing search for food, mainly insects. In some years following very successful breeding seasons, irruptions occur with large numbers arriving from the Continent. At such times strange behaviour such as paper-tearing and milk-bottle opening increases. The Blue Tit is quite an aggressive bird and will evict other small birds from their nest sites, though it never comes off best when contending with a Great Tit.

Voice It has a considerable variety of call notes, but most frequent is a 'tsee, tsee, tsee' often followed by a scolding 'churr'. The song is a rapid liquid trilling following on from its call note.

Habitat Woodland, preferably deciduous, gardens, orchards, hedgerows or anywhere with bushes and trees.

Nest In holes in trees or walls. Often in pipes, gate posts, road signs or letter boxes, and it readily accepts nest boxes. The material used is mainly moss, with a lining of hair, wool and feathers. The 7 to 14 eggs are laid in April or May, white sometimes speckled with reddish-brown but often unmarked. One brood.

Status Resident. A widely distributed bird throughout Britain and Ireland, though it does not breed in the Orkneys or Shetlands. It has increased in recent years, the provision of many more nest boxes no doubt contributing to this in suburban areas. The British and Irish population probably exceeds 5,000,000 pairs.

R.A.H. '79

Great Tit
Parus major ♂

Characteristics 5½in (140mm). As familiar as the Blue Tit, this largest member of the tit tribe is equally engaging and acrobatic, regularly frequenting gardens where it delights the observer with its antics as it feeds on nuts or suet put out for it. Its more natural diet comprises insects, spiders, earthworms, some seeds and buds. It has also been known to kill young fledglings. A handsome bird and easy to identify, with glossy black head and neck, strikingly white cheeks, yellowish-green upper-parts and a broad black band down the centre of the bright yellow under-parts. Males are usually much brighter than females, with richer yellow under-parts; the male's cap also tends to be glossy, not dull-looking, while the black stripe down its middle is much wider. Young birds look like washed-out versions of the adults. Parties of these birds are a feature of autumn woodland, often associating with other tits and small birds.

Voice An extremely varied and extensive repertoire. Two of its commoner notes are a Chaffinch-like 'pink-pink' and a nasal 'tcharr-tcharr'. The song is the familiar 'teacher-teacher-teacher' heard regularly from January to mid-June.

Habitat Deciduous and mixed woodland in the main, but also frequents orchards, hedgerows and gardens.

Nest Typically in a hole in a tree or wall, but it has been recorded nesting in all sorts of openings, from letter boxes to street lamps. It readily takes to nest boxes. Material used is mainly moss and some grass, with a thick layer of hair or down. The 5 to 12 eggs are white with variable red-brown spots, laid April to May. One brood.

Status A resident, generally distributed throughout Britain and Ireland. It has spread into northern areas of Scotland in recent times, but is still sparse in some Highland areas and absent from the Orkneys and Shetlands. The Outer Hebrides have only been colonised in the last few years. The total British and Irish population is around 3 million pairs.

(left) Male; (right) female

163

Nuthatch
Sitta europaea

Characteristics 5½in (140mm). This gravity-defying bird moves down a tree head-first as easily as it moves upwards, clinging to the bark with its powerful feet. It will negotiate any overhang with alacrity and continue its progress in a series of jerky movements along the branch, upside-down if necessary. During the course of the acrobatic performance it does not use its tail as a prop, like a woodpecker or Treecreeper, which makes its performance even more amazing. A large part of this bird's diet consists of nuts, and to get at the kernel it firmly wedges them into a crevice and hacks them open with its pointed woodpecker-like bill, each blow being delivered with the force of the whole body behind it. The bird's presence can often be detected by its loud tappings, and when located it will be seen that the upper-parts are blue-grey with a black stripe through the eye, while the under-parts are buffish and the flanks a rich chestnut colour.

Voice A loud metallic 'chwit-chwit-chwit' and a ringing boyish whistle are the most frequently uttered notes. It also has a loud trilling call.

Habitat Woodland, parks and large gardens, particularly those with ageing deciduous trees. It is rarely encountered in conifers.

Nest In a cavity, often an old woodpecker hole or knot-hole in a trunk. Sometimes in a wall. Uniquely among British birds it reduces the size of the entrance with mud. It will use nest boxes. The inside is lined with flakes of bark and dried leaves. The 6 to 9 eggs are white, usually heavily marked with dark red-brown, laid April to May. One brood.

Status A resident, mainly south of a line from the Dee to the Wash, but absent from large areas of the E Midlands. Not found in Ireland. Breeding population is about 20,000 pairs.

Treecreeper
Certhia familiaris

Characteristics 5in (127mm). A small brown bird with whitish under-parts and a decurved bill, it looks very mouse-like as it ascends the trunk of a tree searching for food, moving upwards and sometimes sideways in a series of little jerks. Having explored the potential of a particular tree it will fly to the base of another nearby to begin the process all over again. It climbs with feet wide apart, body against the trunk and stiff tail feathers held woodpecker-style, providing support. Small insects and grubs are levered from crevices in the bark, while on occasions it will cling tit-like to foliage to pick off insects. Though not a gregarious species it is often to be seen in association with roaming bands of titmice and goldcrests during the winter. It has an interesting roosting behaviour, not keeping only to natural holes or crevices but frequently excavating a hollow in the soft fibrous bark of a Wellingtonia tree where it will spend the night.

Voice A high-pitched 'tsuu' or 'tsit'. The song is a succession of high-pitched notes, starting slowly and accelerating: 'tsee-tsee-tsee-tsizzi-tsee'. It is often delivered whilst climbing. The Treecreeper can be heard regularly from February to May and irregularly at other times.

Habitat Mature woodlands, parks and gardens with plenty of trees. At times it is also found along hedgerows or in conifers.

Nest Built of twigs, moss, roots and grass with a lining of feathers, bark, wool and hair, usually sited behind a loose piece of bark or in a crack, in a stem, or behind ivy. The 5 to 6 eggs are white with small red-brown markings at the large end, laid April to June. Sometimes two broods.

Status A resident, generally distributed throughout Britain where suitable habitat occurs, but absent from the Fens, mountainous areas of Scotland, the Orkneys and Shetlands, and scarcer in Ireland. The estimated population is between 150,000 and 300,000 pairs. Its numbers are much reduced after a hard winter.

Similar or Allied Species The Short-toed Treecreeper (*Certhia brachydactyla*) is very similar but has brownish flanks (not white). The voice is also different. A rare visitor from the Continent. A Schedule I bird.

Treecreeper

165

Red-backed Shrike
Lanius collurio ♂

Characteristics 6¾in (171mm). Sometimes referred to as the butcher-bird, it has the unsavoury habit of impaling its prey, small birds, mammals or insects, on thorns or even barbed wire, forming so-called 'larders'. To secure its food it makes a sudden swooping dive from some exposed vantage point, though on occasions it will hunt along a hedgerow in hawk-like fashion. At times it will also hover while searching for, or before pouncing on, some unsuspecting beetle or other large insect. The male has a red-brown back, blue-grey head with a broad black mark through the eye, grey rump and tail which has white sides, its under-parts being pinkish. The female lacks the black face mask and the back and tail are rufous-brown. Dark crescent-like markings show on the buffish under-parts. Juvenile birds are orangey-brown with dark crescent-shaped markings. When moving from bush to bush it flies with a characteristic upward swoop to its new perch, and when settled the tail is frequently fanned and swung from side to side.

Voice A harsh 'chack-chack' when alarmed, but it has numerous other notes. The song is a subdued warbling which includes some mimicry. Frequently heard from May to July.

Habitat Heaths, commons, downland, open bushy areas, overgrown gardens, disused quarries and railway cuttings.

Nest Built of moss, grass, stalks, wool and feathers, neatly lined with fine roots and hair; it looks like a small Blackbird's nest, and is usually situated in a bramble or overgrown hedge. The eggs, 3 to 6, are variable — pinkish, greenish, yellowish, buffish or combinations of these tones, spotted, blotched and speckled with reddish, greyish or brownish markings — laid May to June. One brood.

Status A summer visitor, arriving April to May and returning September, some birds lingering until October. It has declined markedly in recent years and is now only to be found breeding locally in East Anglia and SE England. Now probably under 50 pairs. Does not breed in Ireland. A Schedule I bird.

Similar or Allied Species The Great Grey Shrike *(Lanius excubitor)* is a passage migrant and winter visitor. Distinctively black, white and grey, it has a long tail which is frequently waved and fanned. It feeds in similar fashion to the Red-backed Shrike but more exclusively on small birds.

Great Grey Shrike

Jay
Garrulus glandarius

Characteristics 13½in (343mm). This colourful member of the crow family is the most arboreal. Generally shy and wary, it often shows no more than a white rump and a flash of bright blue on the wings as it disappears into the depths of a wood, calling harshly as it goes. When seen well, the white and black crest is apparent and is constantly raised and lowered, whilst the tail is fanned and elevated or swung from side to side. The Jay jumps rather clumsily from branch to branch, always on the look-out for danger or the next meal. It is partial to acorns and in autumn spends a great deal of time on the ground collecting and burying these for consumption at a later date. In spring it is an inveterate egg thief, for which reason it is much persecuted in areas where game is reared and often features prominently on keepers' gibbets. It will also raid gardens to take peas and fruit, but on the other hand it does destroy some pests, such as wireworms and the grubs of the destructive winter moth. Its flight appears weak and laboured, with a quick jerky action of its rounded wings.

Voice A harsh 'skark, skark'. It also has a prolonged mewing note.

Habitat Deciduous woodland, particularly oak, but also more open areas with plenty of tree cover.

Nest Built of sticks and twigs, lined with roots and sometimes hair. Situated in fork of tree or bush usually around 15-20ft (5-6m) above ground. The 5 to 6 eggs are greenish-buff with close dark mottling, laid in May. One brood.

Status Present throughout the year, being generally distributed and locally abundant in England and Wales. In Scotland it breeds in parts of the Highlands, but is absent from some S Scottish counties. In Ireland widely distributed except in the S and W. The total British and Irish population is around 100,000 pairs.

Magpie
Pica pica

Characteristics 18in (457mm). A most distinctive bird; its black and white plumage and long wedge-shaped tail identify it immediately, even at long distances. But in order to appreciate the iridescent blue and green of the wings and the purple gloss of the tail it has to be seen at close quarters. Like other members of the crow family, when on the ground it usually walks, but when attracted by some object it hops quickly to investigate, with a sideways motion, wings slightly open and tail elevated. Its choice of food is wide: insects, small mammals, carrion and vegetable matter of all sorts. The eggs and young of other species are also readily taken, which has earned it the dislike of birdlovers and gamekeepers alike. Where it is not persecuted, however, it shows little fear of man though it always remains a wary bird. The flight is direct and slow, but with fairly rapid wing-beats. Magpies tend to follow one behind the other when in groups. Concentrations occur in the early part of the year, when pairing takes place.

Voice A harsh chattering 'aah-aah-aah-aah'.

Nest A fortress-like construction of twigs with a lining of earth, over which is a layer of fine roots and grass. A canopy of sticks gives a domed appearance. Normally situated in the tops of tall hedgerows or single isolated bushes or trees. The 5 to 7 eggs are greenish or yellowish, stongly marked with brown and grey, laid April. One brood.

Status Resident, generally distributed and locally numerous in England and Wales, though scarce in parts of East Anglia and rare or absent from large areas of Scotland. Widespread in Ireland. Total population of Britain and Ireland probably over 250,000 pairs.

Chough

Pyrrhocorax pyrrhocorax

Characteristics 15in (381mm). Of all the members of the crow family this rare bird is probably the most exciting to birdwatchers. Perhaps it is because it inhabits some of Britain's most spectacular cliff scenery that it is so highly regarded, and also its purplish-black plumage, curved red bill and red legs are striking. It is certainly more graceful in flight than the Jackdaw, to which it approximates in size. It progresses with a series of leisurely flaps and glides, primaries widely separated, their tips often curving upwards. It can often be seen performing aerial acrobatics about cliff faces and frequently soars. A noisy and sociable bird, it is to be found in small groups searching the short turfy grass of cliff tops for ants and their larvae, particularly, as well as other insects. At other times it forages along the shore, picking up small molluscs and crustacea. On the ground it walks, runs and hops and when it calls has the habit of flirting its tail and wing tips.

Voice Very Jackdaw-like, but more musical and slightly more drawn out—an explosive 'pee-yah'.

Habitat Mainly rugged coastal areas, but also mountainous areas inland.

Nest A substantial structure of heather, sticks or other plant stalks, lined with wool or hair with some grass and feathers, typically situated in a cliff crevice or sea cave; inland, similar sites on rock faces and quarries are selected. The 3 to 5 eggs are pale yellowish-white, mottled with brown and grey, laid April onwards. One brood.

Status A resident, whose numbers have greatly declined in recent years; it is now restricted to Ireland, the Isle of Man, parts of Wales and SW Scotland. Probably there are fewer than 1,000 pairs, most of them in Ireland. A Schedule I bird.

Jackdaw
Corvus monedula

Characteristics 13in (330mm). The thieving habits of the crow family are well known and this species particularly has a reputation for stealing, being bold in its quest for bright objects. There are many tales of lost treasure being retrieved from Jackdaws' nests, mostly in fable, as chronicled in *The Jackdaw of Rheims*. Often kept as pets, they become totally unafraid of man, and if allowed to roam freely in a surburban setting, soon get into trouble: many a line of washing has suffered from a Jackdaw's attentions. Frequently found in the company of Rooks, it is quickly singled out by its much smaller size, faster flight with quicker wing beats and almost pigeon-like action. On the ground it walks with a quick jaunty air, poking and picking for all manner of food, including worms, insects, slugs, snails, cereals, fruits and berries. It also takes young birds, eggs and small mammals. At close quarters the black plumage can be seen to be glossed with blue on the head and upper-parts, though it is the grey nape which is distinctive. The eye is noticeably greyish-white in the adult, blue in the young birds.

Voice An unmistakable 'chack'; also 'kyaah'.

Habitat Open woodland especially with old timber, also parkland, old ruins, quarries, coastal or inland cliffs. It forages in fields.

Nest A foundation of sticks and all kinds of rubbish, with a lining of wool, sometimes hair, fur, etc. Normally in a hole or cavity in a tree, building or cliff; frequently in chimneys, lofts, etc. The 4 to 6 eggs are light blue-green with dark brown spots or streaks, laid April. One brood.

Status A common resident, widely distributed throughout Britain and Ireland, but scarce in NW Scotland. It breeds sporadically in the Outer Hebrides and Shetlands. The British and Irish population is around 500,000 pairs.

Rook

Corvus frugilegus

Characteristics 18in (457mm). This species and the next are large black birds and easily confused. There is an old country saying that 'one Rook is a Crow and a flock of Crows are Rooks'! Though there is some substance in this maxim, Rooks being highly gregarious and the Carrion Crow a comparatively solitary species, it is not a totally reliable means of distinguishing them, and other points need to be looked for. One of the most obvious differences is the greyish patch of bare skin on this bird's face, readily seen at rest or in flight. Young birds do not have this however, and somewhat resemble the Carrion Crow; but the more slender bill, and the loose feathers about the flanks which give a 'baggy-trousers' appearance at all ages, should serve to separate the two species. Rooks are also most often to be seen in the fields, sometimes several hundred strong, moving about with a sedate walk and an occasional hop, probing here and digging there, searching for worms, leatherjackets or other insect larvae. Cereal roots and other vegetable matter are also taken. The flight is slow and deliberate, flocks flying in loose straggling formations. In winter Rooks roost together, usually near a rookery, often with Jackdaws.

Voice Most well known note is a 'caw' or 'kaah'.

Habitat Agricultural country with suitable stands of trees for nesting, frequenting both pasture and arable land. Associated with human settlement, but on occasions found in more remote areas.

Nest A bulky, untidy structure of twigs, lined with grass, leaves, roots, etc. Situated in the tops of tall trees, colonies are used year after year. Will nest in lower trees or bushes, exceptionally on church spires, chimneys and electricity pylons. The 4 to 6 eggs are bluish-green to greyish-green, heavily marked with brown spots and blotches, laid March to April. One brood.

Status Resident, being generally distributed throughout England and Ireland. However, Rooks are scarce in central Wales and on the Scottish border, in SW and NW Scotland and the Scottish islands. Numbers have declined in recent years. Total population estimated at 1½ million pairs.

Carrion Crow
Corvus corone corone

Characteristics 18½in (470mm). In a good light the all-black plumage shows a metallic sheen, having a greener look than the Rook's purplish gloss. However, the heavy black bill and lack of a bare face patch are this bird's major distinguishing features. Also its neater, more compact, appearance, should help identify it. Like other Crows it is a ground feeder, walking or hopping with equal ease, taking a wide variety of foods, from grain, vegetable matter, insects and worms to small birds, eggs, small mammals and amphibians, with a partiality for carrion of all sorts. It will also feed along the shoreline and will smash crabs and molluscs by dropping them from a height. The flight is slower and more deliberate than the Rook's and the tail is square-ended.

Voice A deep 'karr', also a repetitive 'car-horn' note delivered when the bird is perched, lunging forward each time it calls.

Habitat All sorts of country, from open moorland to well-wooded and cultivated areas. Also found along the coast, in towns and cities and on derelict land.

Nest Built of sticks, earth, moss, etc, lined with hair and wool, chiefly in a fork or the upper branches of a tree, but it may be quite low down in a bush, and cliff sites are used on the coast. The 4 to 6 eggs are light blue or green, covered with brown spots and blotches, like small Raven's eggs, laid April onwards. One brood.

Status A resident, widely found throughout England and Wales. In NW Scotland, Ireland and the Isle of Man the Hooded Crow (*Corvus cornix*) takes over. There is a narrow area of overlap in Scotland where interbreeding takes place. Total population about 1 million, with over half of these Carrion Crows.

Similar or Allied Species The Hooded Crow (*Corvus corone cornix*) is similar in size, shape, voice and habits, but differs in plumage; its grey back and under-parts are most distinctive.

Hooded Crow

Raven

Corvus corax

Characteristics 25in (635mm). The largest and most powerful of the crows, and size alone should quickly distinguish it from the Carrion Crow. Additionally the stouter bill and distinctive wedge-shaped tail are aids to identification. Most frequently and easily seen in flight, it often soars to a great height on motionless wings, flight feathers extended like fingers on a hand; at other times it will perform aerial acrobatics, particularly during the breeding season, when it will roll, swoop and dive, calling as it does so. On the ground it walks and hops rather clumsily, compared to its aerial dexterity. It perches freely on crags or trees, as available, from where it will call, lunging forward with each note, the shaggy throat-feathers showing prominently. A pair will stay together throughout the year, while in areas where it is numerous small parties forage and roost together. Food is varied, but its habit of feeding on carrion has often brought it under suspicion of killing new-born lambs, though there is rarely the evidence to support this belief.

Voice Usual notes are a deep 'pruk, pruk' in flight and a throaty 'grok'.

Habitat Mountainous or hilly districts, moorland, coastal areas; also occurs in wooded lowlands in places.

Nest A bulky structure of sticks reinforced with mud, often attaining huge proportions, being added to year after year. Lining usually wool and hair. Situated on a cliff ledge or frequently in a tree. The 4 to 6 eggs are light blue to greenish, liberally marked with brown spots and blotches, laid February to March. One brood.

Status A resident, found in Scotland (though scarce or absent in the NE), parts of NE England, the Isle of Man, most of Wales and SW England. Widely scattered in Ireland, mainly round coastal areas. British and Irish population is about 5,000 pairs.

Starling
Sturnus vulgaris

W

Characteristics 8½in (216mm). This ubiquitous bird is at home anywhere, though its presence is more readily noted in towns and cities, particularly when it gathers to roost during the winter. Though noisy and messy, fouling buildings and pavements, a flock of these birds makes an impressive spectacle as they wheel and circle, often in their thousands, eventually to settle in a fluttering, twittering black mass on the buildings of their choice. In full breeding dress the black plumage is glossed bronze-green and purple, long sharp bill is yellow and the legs pinkish. In winter it has a spangled appearance, more marked in the female, and the bill is dark. Young birds are mouse-brown and as they moult show varying degrees of juvenile plumage and winter dress. On the ground Starlings rush about with a quick jerky walk or run to investigate something which attracts their attention. When feeding on grass it pecks with the beak open. Its food is mainly insects, but it also eats a variety of other items, including household scraps. Flight is fast and direct on short pointed wings, which, with its plump form and short tail, give it a distinctive appearance both in the air and when settled.

Voice The call is a grating 'tcheer'. The song is a mixture of whistles, clicks and chuckles with the calls of many other birds mixed in, for the Starling is an accomplished mimic. As it sings from some prominent position the head is held up, the throat feathers are distended and the wings trail. It sings most months of the year, but more regularly in August to May.

Habitat Town and country.

Nest A mixture of straw and feathers located in natural holes or cavities, or in a building, especially under eaves; the Starling will take over the hole of other nesting birds. It readily uses nest boxes. The 4 to 7 eggs are pale blue, laid April onwards. One brood, sometimes two.

Status Present throughout the year, and generally distributed in every part of Britain and Ireland. There is considerable immigration from the Continent in autumn. The total breeding population is estimated at 7 million pairs.

174

House Sparrow
Passer domesticus ♂

Characteristics 5¾in (146mm). The Speug or English Sparrow, as it is sometimes called, is one of our most familiar birds. Its very existence seems to depend on man, his husbandry and his wasteful activities. When not soiled by city dirt, the male Sparrow is quite a smart little bird, with white cheeks, grey crown and black bib, brown and black upper-parts, and whitish under-parts. The hen, however, is much drabber-looking, with a buff and black streaked back and none of the male's distinctive markings. Gregarious at all seasons, by their very abundance Sparrows tend to be a bit of a nuisance, and are accused of all manner of sins. They certainly devour large quantities of grain and will attack most cultivated berry fruits. Fruit-tree buds are eaten and it has the annoying habit of nipping the tops of ornamental plants as they come through in spring; many a good showing of crocuses has been ruined. Yet one cannot but admire the bird's opportunism.

Voice The loud 'cheep' is as well known as its appearance. It also has various other twittering and chirping notes.

Habitat Towns and villages, farms, anywhere near to human habitation.

Nest An untidy domed structure of straw and grass, lined with feathers and wool, sometimes with other material oddments included. It is situated in almost any kind of hole or cavity, often in lofts where the heaps of nesting material can be huge. The bird sometimes builds in the base of Rooks' and Herons' nests; it will use nest boxes and sometimes takes over House Martins' nests. Occasionally it nests in an open situation, such as a hedge or bush. The 3 to 5 eggs are variable, off-white, speckled and blotched with shades of grey. Though eggs have been found in almost every month, they are generally laid in May to August. Three broods are quite frequent.

Status A resident, widely distributed in Britain and Ireland and only absent from high exposed areas. The estimated breeding population is around 5 million pairs.

Female

Tree Sparrow
Passer montanus

Characteristics 5½in (140mm). Very similar to the House Sparrow, this charming little bird is frequently overlooked. When seen feeding with House Sparrows, close scrutiny will reveal a neater, trimmer appearance with the whole of the cap a rich chestnut, the white face showing a black patch on the ear coverts. The double, white wing bar is another feature to look for, as it is not immediately apparent. The sexes are alike and the young resemble adults. Shy and unobtrusive, it is often noticed only when winter flocks roam the countryside unless the distinctive call note is known.

Voice A persistent 'chip-chip' note, higher-pitched than the House Sparrow's. Also has a rather hoarse 'tek-tek' flight note.

Habitat A more rural species than the House Sparrow, frequenting hedgerows, old orchards, edges of woodland, pollarded willows, etc.

Nest Built of straw and grass, similar to House Sparrow's but neater. Normally located in a hole or crevice in a building or tree, but will use nest boxes. In April lays 4 to 6 eggs, smaller than the House Sparrow's, darker and browner. Two broods, sometimes three.

Status Resident, locally common, but scarce or absent from NW Scotland, parts of NW Scotland, parts of NW England, western parts of Wales, SW England, Hampshire and Sussex. In Ireland the scattered colonies are mainly coastal. Total population of Britain and Ireland about 250,000 pairs.

176

Chaffinch
Fringilla coelebs ♂

Characteristics 6in (152mm). Our commonest finch, the male particularly is a distinctive bird with his slate-blue crown, chestnut-brown back and pinkish under-parts. However, when at rest the most notable feature is the broad white shoulder patch with a less prominent white wing bar behind it. In flight these show as a distinct double wing bar, which, with the greenish rump and black tail with white outer feathers, gives markings like no other European finch. The female lacks the male's brighter colours though she has similar markings and looks very greenish on the back in flight. Juveniles are like females, but are less green on the rump. In winter the Chaffinch associates with other finches, roaming the countryside in large flocks with the Brambling a frequent companion. Seeds of many kinds are eaten, also some insects, spiders and small worms. It flies in the undulating manner typical of the finch family.

Voice A metallic 'chwink-chwink' which has given rise to the local name of Spink. In spring a characteristic clear loud 'wheet'. The flight note is 'tsup'. The song is a cheery short vigorous rattling succession of rather unmusical notes usually terminating in a flourish. This has been rendered 'You naughty little boy I'm going to beat you!' Song starts in March but the complete version is not usually heard until April and then through to June.

Habitat In the breeding season, deciduous and coniferous woodland, hedgerows and other places with suitable cover. Outside the breeding season, arable and pasture land, stubble and root fields, stack yards and any place where grain or seeds can be found.

Nest A neat compact cup of moss, grass, wool and roots decorated with lichens held in place with spiders' webs, lined with hair and the odd feather. Usually in a bush or the fork of a small tree, particularly hawthorn, but a wide variety of other settings are chosen. The 4 to 5 eggs are blue or light brown with a few smudgy spots and streaks of dark brown, laid April to May. One brood.

Status Present throughout the year. A widely distributed and abundant bird, but scarce in the Hebrides and Orkneys. It does not breed in the Shetlands. Total population of Britain and Ireland estimated at around 7 million pairs.

(left) Female ; (right) male

Brambling
Fringilla montifringilla   ♀

Characteristics 5¾in (146mm). A frequent companion of Chaffinches in winter, and mixed flocks are often to be found feeding in the open fields or under beech trees where fallen beechmast is a favourite food. Against a background of fallen leaves they are extremely difficult to see, their grey-brown, orange-buff and black plumage blending perfectly with the woodland floor. If disturbed, however, flight reveals a white rump and a bold pattern of orange-buff shoulder patches (in the male) and white bars in the wing, but unlike the Chaffinch the Brambling has no white in the tail. When migrant birds arrive in the autumn, some males still have the glossy black head of summer plumage, but as winter progresses this becomes mottled brown. The head often becomes black again however before their departure in spring.

Voice The usual note is a hoarse metallic 'tsweek'; in flight a rapid 'chucc-chucc-chucc'. The song is a Greenfinch-like 'zwee' with a few rapidly repeated chirpy notes included.

Habitat Woods, particularly beech, stack yards and open fields.

Status Mainly a winter visitor, with numbers varying considerably: common in some years and scarce in others. Singing and displaying males noted more frequently in recent years and sporadic breeding may be taking place. The only confirmed breeding record was in Sutherland in 1920. A Schedule I bird.

Male, summer plumage

Greenfinch
Carduelis chloris ♂

Characteristics 5¾in (146mm). In breeding plumage the male is olive-green, but at certain times of year it hardly lives up to its name, looking greyish. But whatever the stage of moult, the bright yellow patches on the primaries and the sides of the tail are always diagnostic. The female is duller-looking at all times, the juveniles are browner and streaked, both being easily mistaken for House Sparrows if given only a cursory glance. In flight the Greenfinch looks plump and rather short-bodied with a distinctly cleft tail. Like other finches it is a sociable species, and flocks from autumn through to spring, often with other finches, foraging for seeds and waste grain. Many visit gardens, feeding on nuts put out for titmice, a habit they have acquired only in recent years. In spring the male proclaims his presence with a distinctive display flight, circling over the tree tops with slow flapping wings, calling as he goes.

Voice A loud rapid trill, also a short 'chup' or 'teu'. In spring and autumn the Greenfinch frequently utters a nasal 'zwee'. The song is a canary-like twitter with call notes mixed in, regularly heard from March to July.

Habitat In the breeding season, hedgerows, gardens, parks, open scrubby bushy areas. In winter, fields, stack yards, waste ground.

Nest Built of twigs, grass and moss, it is lined with roots and hair, sometimes some feathers. It is usually sited in a hedgerow or bush. The 4 to 6 eggs are off-white, sparsely streaked and spotted with red-brown, laid late April to early May. Two broods, occasionally three.

Status A resident, widely distributed, but sparse or absent from N and W Scotland, the Shetlands and parts of Wales. Total population of Britain and Ireland between 1 million and 2 million pairs.

Goldfinch
Carduelis carduelis

Characteristics 4¾in (121mm). Our most colourful finch, immediately recognisable by its striking red, white and black head, boldly marked black and yellow wings, black and white tail and white rump. The sexes are alike and while the juvenile lacks the bright face pattern it has the same yellow markings on the wings. A seed-eater, it particularly favours thistles and any patch of these will attract a 'charm' of these delightful birds. In such circumstances it can be seen hanging, titlike, pulling out the downy-topped seed heads with its sharply pointed bill. This specialised bill enables it to tackle groundsel, dandelion, burdock and teasels with equal dexterity. Despite its skill, there are occasions when birds have been trapped by the barbed hooks of teasel heads. In spring it performs a display flight similar to that of the Greenfinch. It is equally sociable and is often to be found in quite sizeable flocks, but generally it does not mix so readily with other finches.

Voice A conversational twitter uttered during feeding and on the wing, with a tinkling bell-like quality. The song is a clear, sweet, liquid twitter, regularly heard from March to July and occasionally at other times of the year.

Habitat In the breeding season, gardens, orchards and open cultivated land. In autumn and winter it is found on waste land and any open areas where weeds occur.

Nest A neat compact Chaffinch-like nest of grass, moss, lichens and wool, lined with vegetable down and wool; hair is also used. The favourite site is the fork of a horizontal branch of a fruit tree. The 5 to 6 bluish-white eggs have spots and streaks of dark chestnut-brown, laid April to May. Two broods, occasionally three.

Status A resident, generally distributed throughout Britain and Ireland, but sparse in N England and the Scottish lowlands. Scarce or totally absent in N Scotland, the Hebrides, Orkneys and Shetlands. Total population probably around 300,000 pairs.

Siskin
Carduelis spinus ♂

Characteristics 4¾in (121mm). This active little bird is as acrobatic as a tit, spending much time hanging upside-down picking at alder cones or birch seeds, particularly in winter. Its fortunes appear to be linked with those of the spruce tree, and it flourishes in seasons with a good crop of spruce seeds. The male is predominantly yellow-green with a black crown and chin and yellow rump. The wings are relatively long for the size of the bird and show bright yellow bars in flight. The male also has yellow patches either side of the forked tail. The female has no black cap or chin and is greyer-looking and more streaky underneath, but shares the same wing pattern. Generally keeping to the tops of trees, they occasionally feed on the ground. Flight is fast, with typical finch action. Gregarious in winter, the Siskin frequently consorts with Redpolls.

Voice Flocks maintain a constant twitter. Its distinctive call notes are a squeaky 'tsy-zing' and a wheezy 'tsooeet'. The song is a simple twittering, ending with a prolonged creaky note, usually uttered during the display flight, but also when perched. It is mainly heard from mid-February to the end of April.

Habitat In the breeding season, coniferous woodland, especially spruce. Also mixed woodland, parks and gardens where conifers are found. In winter it frequents birch and alder trees, often along the course of a stream. Since around 1963 numbers of Siskins have visited suburban gardens, feeding on nuts put out for tits. This activity has been observed mostly in February, March and April, and nuts in red plastic bags have been said to be preferred to those in other types of container!

Nest Built of small lichen-covered twigs with moss and wool, it is lined with roots, hair and some feathers. It is usually placed in horizontal branches of pine, spruce, fir or larch, often at a great height. The 4 to 5 eggs are pale blue with red-brown spots and fine streaks, laid in April. Two broods.

Status Breeds widely in N Scotland and at scattered localities elsewhere in Britain, particularly where suitable conifer plantations occur. In Ireland it is mainly found in the SW, SE, NW and parts of Ulster. The estimated breeding population of Britain and Ireland is around 40,000 pairs. It is also a winter visitor, arriving in September, leaving in March and April. A Schedule I bird.

Similar or Allied Species The Serin (*Serinus serinus*) is another small yellowish-looking finch. The male has a bright yellow forehead. Common on the Continent, it is a rare visitor to Britain, but has nested here. A Schedule I bird.

Male Siskin

Linnet

Acanthis cannabina ♂

Characteristics 5¼in (133mm). In breeding dress the cock is an attractive bird, and as it also has a pleasant little song it is not surprising that it was a popular cage bird in the nineteenth century. The back is a warm chestnut-brown, the under-parts shading from fawn to almost white. The head is greyish-brown, and the forehead, crown and breast are crimson, which distinguishes it from the female. Young birds are duller-looking and more heavily streaked. Its food consists mainly of weed seeds, including such favourites as thistle, charlock, dandelion and dock. Cultivated crops such as turnip and oilseed rape are also attractive. The young in the nest are fed on regurgitated seed. The species is highly gregarious, and large flocks, sometimes of 1,000 birds or more, gather in autumn. Winter roosts can also be considerable. Though Linnets have not normally visited gardens, there are indications this habit may be developing.

Voice Flight note is a rapid twittering. Usual call 'tsooeet'. The song is a simple, sweet twanging musical twitter with an occasional harsh note mixed in. Mainly heard from late March to mid-July.

Habitat In the breeding season, open bushy country, gorsy commons, young conifer plantations and hedgerows. Also coastal regions with suaeda, sea buckthorn and other bushes. In winter it roams waste ground, farmland, marshes, etc.

Nest Mainly constructed of stalks and grass stems, sometimes small twigs, it is lined with wool, hair and sometimes feathers. Usually in a bush, traditionally gorse, but also in bramble or thorn. It is often a colonial nester, with several pairs in close proximity. The 4 to 6 eggs are pale blue with dark brown spots and streaks, laid April to May. Two, sometimes three, broods.

Status Present throughout the year. A common, widely distributed breeding bird, but local and scarce in the Highlands and NW Scotland. Scarce in the Hebrides. Breeds in the Orkneys, but absent from the Shetlands. Sparse in parts of Ulster. Total population of Britain and Ireland probably 1½ million pairs.

Similar or Allied Species The Twite (*Acanthis flavirostris*) is a small Linnet-type bird but without the crimson breeding plumage. The male is distinguished by a pink rump and yellow bill and a different call, a nasal 'chweer'. The female has the yellow beak but no pink rump. A bird of moorland areas, it is sometimes called the Mountain Linnet. It breeds locally in the Pennines and NW Scotland, the Hebrides, Orkney and the Shetlands. Some nest in coastal areas of W Ireland. It winters on salt marshes, also stubble fields and waste ground, usually near the coast. A Schedule I bird.

(left) Linnet; (right) Twite

Redpoll
Acanthis flammea   ♀

Characteristics 4¾in (121mm). There is some similarity between this bird and the Linnet, but it is much smaller and darker-looking. The adult has a crimson forehead, but the chin is black, distinguishing it at once; additionally, the underparts are whitish with a pinkish tinge to the upper breast. There are also two quite distinctive buff-coloured wing bars. Young birds have no red cap or black bib, but their parents are likely to be seen hanging from some branch or twig of a riverside alder feeding on the seeds (often in the company of Siskins), an unlikely setting for the Linnet. In spring the Redpoll advertises its presence by flying round in a circular display song flight with slow deliberate wing-beats. It also sings in direct flight (the usual undulating finch action) or from some favourite perch.

Voice The flight note is a distinctive rapid 'chuch-uch-uch-uch'. It also has a plaintive anxiety note. The song is a sustained series of brief trills, interspersed with flight calls.

Habitat In the breeding season, birch wood, areas of alders, coniferous plantations, hedgerows and more recently gardens.

Nest A cup of moss, bark strips and dead leaves on a foundation of twigs and rootlets, lined with white vegetable down and some hair, occasionally a few feathers. It can be low down in a bush or at some height in the fork of a tree. The eggs, 4 to 6, are blue, streaked and spotted with red-brown, laid in April. One, sometimes two, broods

Status Present throughout the year, breeding widely in Scotland, N and E England and in Ireland. Has increased in recent years, spreading into lowland areas of England, but still sparse or local in S Midlands and SW England. The estimated breeding population of Britain and Ireland is around 600,000 pairs.

Similar or Allied Species The Mealy Redpoll (*Acanthis f. flammea*) is a Continental race, which is larger and paler than the Redpoll. The Arctic Redpoll (*Acanthis hornemanni*) is the largest and whitest of the Redpoll group. Both are occasionally recorded in winter.

Redpoll   R.A.A.

Crossbill

Loxia curvirostra   ♂

Characteristics 6½in (165mm). A strange bird whose sporadic occurrence in Britain is only one aspect of its unusual life history. Well known in legend, one of the stories of how it gained its crossed mandibles is that they became distorted during its attempts to wrench the nails from the hands of Christ as He hung from the cross. The curved mandibles which cross at the tips are in fact the perfect tool for extracting seed from fir cones. The bird holds the cone with one foot and then forces the scales apart to get at the fruit, not always easy to see. Crossbills draw attention to themselves by their call note, and also the sound of cone scales being cracked is quite audible; when a large flock is feeding in the top branches of a pine wood, the shower of seed wings and cones which comes floating down is also sufficiently obvious to draw attention to their presence. With experience it is possible to tell whether Crossbills have been in the neighbourhood by examination of fallen cones, as attacks by woodpeckers and squirrels leave quite different traces. In some years large numbers occur, these 'irruptions' being due to food shortage in Europe. Often only the green-grey females and grey-streaked juvenile birds are seen, though there is usually a sprinkling of crimson-coloured males to delight the observer. Males are especially brilliant on the rump.

Voice A loud 'chip, chip'. The song is a rather variable Greenfinch-like trill with call notes mixed in. Frequently heard from mid-January to August.

Habitat Rarely away from coniferous woodland.

Nest A strong foundation of pine twigs with a superstructure of grasses and wool lined with grass, rabbit fur, hair, feathers, etc, somewhat flattened in shape, usually situated in pine trees, often quite high off the ground. The eggs, usually 4, are off-white, spotted and streaked red-brown, indistinguishable from those of the Greenfinch, laid January or February or even as late as July. One brood, occasionally two.

Status Present throughout the year, being resident and indigenous in N Scotland. Scattered breeding in other parts of Britain, particularly in Norfolk Brecklands and the New Forest. Does not breed regularly in Ireland. Total population probably about 5,000 pairs, though following irruptive movements of birds from the Continent there may well be more. A Schedule I bird.

Similar or Allied Species The resident Scottish birds are regarded as a separate species, distinguished by its larger bill, but difficult to identify in the field. Common Crossbills also occur in Scotland, sometimes in the same areas.

Bullfinch
Pyrrhula pyrrhula ♂♀

Characteristics 5¾in (146mm). The male is an exceedingly handsome bird with his reddish-pink breast, blue-grey back and glossy black cap, while the female has the same basic plumage pattern but the colours are brownish. The juvenile is like the female but lacks the black cap. Shy and retiring, Bullfinches are often noticed only if their plaintive call uttered from the depths of some thick hedge is recognised, or when they have attacked fruit blossom. They can cause much damage to fruit crops: one individual has been observed to strip up to 30 buds in a minute. Apples, pears, currants, gooseberries, plums all suffer. Almost certainly Bullfinches pair for life, as through the winter male and female can usually be seen together, flitting along a hedgerow or across some open space with undulating flight when the distinctive white rump can be seen. Family parties are to be noted in late summer and autumn.

Voice A regularly uttered soft piping call. The song is a mixture of warbling and creaking notes, only audible at close range, uttered infrequently between February and August.

Habitat Woods, hedgerows, gardens, orchards, young forestry plantations.

Nest A cup of fine black roots often mixed with hair, on a platform of small twigs. Placed in a thick bush or tree (often evergreen) and commonly in brambles, briars or thorn. The 4 to 6 eggs are greenish-blue with dark purple-brown streaks, laid April to May. Two broods.

Status Resident, widely distributed, but locally scarce or absent from some areas, notably the Highlands, N Scotland, the Hebrides, Orkneys and Shetlands, parts of Central Wales and Northern Ireland. It does not breed in the Isle of Man. Total British and Irish population around 600,000 pairs.

Hawfinch
Coccothraustes coccothraustes   ♂ S

Characteristics 6½in (165mm). This incredible bird with its enormous bill and 'bull-necked' appearance is unmistakable when seen — which is infrequently, for it is extremely secretive and unless the flight call is known often goes undetected. The tawny-coloured head, bluish-grey collar, reddish-brown back and bold white patches on blue-black wings are distinctive enough, even without its huge deep bill which is bluish (horn-coloured) in winter. This powerful tool can even crack open cherry stones as well as damson and sloe stones and hornbeam seeds, one of its favourite foods. In winter hips and haws are also taken and fed to the young. The female is paler-looking, being less rufous on the crown. The juvenile has distinctive crescent markings on the under-parts. In flight the massive head shape is accentuated by the long wings and short tail, and whether seen from above or below the black and white wing pattern is conspicuous. This bird has black, strange-shaped inner primaries, notched and curved, but their purpose is unknown.

Voice A loud explosive 'ptik', somewhat Robin-like. The song is little known and rarely heard.

Habitat In the breeding season, deciduous and mixed woodland, orchards, old wooded gardens. In winter, it collects in small flocks, feeding on the ground in woods or more open country.

Nest A shallow cup of rootlets, lichens and bents, lined with fine roots and hair, on a foundation of small twigs. The usual situation is on a horizontal branch or small fork of a tree, apple and sycamore preferred. The 3 to 6 eggs are bluish-white to brownish-green, blotched, spotted and marked with dark brown, laid in May. One brood.

Status A resident, breeding locally in England and Wales with most records from SE England. Unknown in Devon and Cornwall. A few scattered occurences in Southern Scotland. Absent from Ireland. The bird's elusive habits no doubt explain the patchy distribution records to some extent. The total breeding population is probably less than 10,000 pairs.

Snow Bunting
Plectrophenax nivalis ♂

Characteristics 6½in (165mm). In its summer plumage the male has a pure white head and under-parts, the back and central tail feathers and primaries being black. In flight this contrasting plumage pattern make it a most conspicuous bird, though its breeding grounds are often snow-covered and then it is camouflaged. However, the bold mixture of black and white features prominently in its courtship display, which comprises a number of threat attitudes and singing in upward, wing-trembling flight. The female is not so distinctly marked, having a grey-brown head and back flecked with black. Confined to a limited area of Britain as a breeding bird, it is more familiar as a winter visitor, when its distinctive coloration is a mixture of dull whites and rusty browns. The male, however, still retains the prominent white wing marking, visible in flight and unlike any other bunting. A gregarious species, it spends much time on the ground picking up seeds with its tiny yellow bill. The flight is fast and undulating, birds skimming the ground for several yards before settling.

Voice The usual call is a musical rippling twitter, 'tirrirrirririp'. It also has a loud high-pitched 'tsweet' and plaintive 'teup' and 'teu' notes. The song is a short, musical, almost lark-like warble uttered in flight or on the ground.

Habitat In the breeding season, remote mountainous regions giving tundra-type conditions. In the winter, along seashores and open coastal regions, frequenting salt marshes, stubble fields, etc.

Nest Built of moss and grass, lined with finer stems and often many feathers (mostly Ptarmigan), located in a crevice in a rock or boulder scree. The 4 to 6 eggs are off-white, bluish or greenish marked with dark red-brown spots and blotches with underlying violet marks. Laid in May to June. Two broods usual.

Status Present throughout the year, breeding in N Scotland—mainly centred in the Cairngorms; but probably no more than half a dozen pairs all told. Elsewhere in the British Isles a winter visitor, arriving early September, returning March to mid-May. Mainly found along the coast, sometimes in flocks which may be several hundred strong. A Schedule I bird.

(left) Male; (right) female

Yellowhammer
Emberiza citrinella ♂

Characteristics 6½in (165mm). Less frequently called the Yellow Bunting, this is a familiar bird, if known only for its monotonous song, which can be heard through the summer months when most other species have ceased singing. It sits on top of a hedgerow or bush in full view, when the male can be readily seen to live up to the name, with bright lemon yellow head and under-parts. The yellow head is particularly noticeable even in flight, when additionally the rufous rump and white outer tail feathers distinguish it from all other buntings. The female and juveniles have much less yellow, but the rufous rump and the slimmer look and longish tail, which is continuously flicked, should be sufficient to identify them. It feeds almost exclusively on the ground, picking up corn, seeds and other vegetable matter, also insects, spiders, worms, etc. Gregarious in spring and autumn, it often associates with other buntings and finches.

Voice A distinctive 'chinz' note is frequently uttered. The song is a rattling wheeze, commonly interpreted as 'a little bit of bread and no cheese'. It can be heard regularly from the early part of the year through to August, intermittently until October and occasionally during November.

Habitat Agricultural land, edges of woods, young conifer plantations, heaths, commons, open countryside with bracken cover, bushes, etc, waste and derelict land.

Nest Well built of grass, straw and moss, lined with hair. The typical site is in a bank, below, or at the base of a hedge, or under bramble or dead bracken. The 3 to 5 eggs are whitish with dark scribbling marks, which give rise to the common name Scribbling Lark; laid April or May onwards. Two broods, sometimes three.

Status Present throughout the year. Widely distributed, but only found locally along parts of the Pennines and in the Scottish Highlands. Scarce in the Hebrides and Orkneys. Absent from the Shetlands. Sparse in some areas of Ireland. Total British and Irish populations around 1 million pairs.

Female

Reed Bunting
Emberiza schoeniclus   ♂

Characteristics 6in (152mm). When seen perched on a reed stem or on top of a bush, the black head and throat and white collar of the adult male are conspicuous features. The brown and black streaked back is very Sparrow-like (an old country name is Water Sparrow), but the white outer feathers of the tail, which is constantly flicked, fanned and closed, distinguish it. In winter the head pattern is less pronounced. The female has a distinct black and white moustachial streak, the juvenile being similarly patterned, with the white having a yellowish tinge. With jerky undulating flight it flits from bush to bush and reed to reed, searching for the seeds of marsh plants which form the major part of its diet. It also eats some insects. In winter its breeding haunts are not totally deserted, but some join with other buntings to forage in the fields.

Voice The usual note is a loud 'tseep', also a metallic 'ching'. The alarm note is a sharp 'zit'. The song is a monotonous, tinkling 'tweek-tweek-tweek, tititick', and is heard regularly from March to July or August.

Habitat In the breeding season, usually watery settings, such as reed beds, rushy meadows, the margins of lakes and streams. In recent years, it has also been found in drier situations. In winter, cultivated fields, open ground and gardens are increasingly frequented.

Nest Built of dry grass and sedges lined with grass and some hair, it is usually sited in tussocks of reed or grass on or near the ground. Increasingly found in small conifers, hedgerows, gorse, etc. The 4 to 5 eggs are olive-brown or buff with dark streaks and spots, laid April or May. Two broods, sometimes three.

Status Present throughout the year and widely distributed, though absent from upland regions including parts of SW England, the Cotswolds, Snowdonia, the Lake District and the Scottish Highlands. Estimated breeding population of Britain and Ireland around 600,000 pairs.

Female

Corn Bunting
Miliaria calandra

Characteristics 7in (178mm). This drab-looking bird lacks any outstanding plumage features, though close inspection reveals an overall pattern of short dark streaks on the brown upper-parts. The pale under-parts are also streaked, but mainly round the upper breast, resembling a necklace. Largest of the buntings, it

looks a bulky, heavy-bodied bird, especially in flight. When leaving a song post it has a distinctive habit of dangling its legs as it flies low over the ground. Though it perches freely on telegraph wires and bushes, it is not often seen in trees. A ground feeder, picking up all manner of seeds, it occasionally takes buds and corn, and also a deal of animal matter, mostly insects. Gregarious in winter, often found in the company of other buntings. The sexes are similar.

Voice A loud abrupt 'quit' or 'quit-it-it' in flight. The song is a short sequence of ticking notes leading to a discordant finish likened to the jangling of a bunch of keys. This may be regularly heard from February through to August.

Habitat In the breeding season, arable grassland, cultivated areas with a few trees, commons, downland, rough pastures, scrubby areas near the coast. In winter, cultivated land, stack yards, etc.

Nest Built of grasses, lined with finer grass, especially with clumps of thistle and knapweed, etc, also in hedges and occasionally in crops. The 3 to 5 eggs are greyish-white to light brown with blackish-brown scribbling marks, blotches, streaks and spots, laid in late May. One or two broods usual.

Status Present throughout the year, but having a most irregular breeding distribution, being absent from much of the SW and N England, Wales, large areas of Scotland, Ireland and Isle of Man. Most widespread in England but missing from parts of East Anglia and the Weald of Sussex and Kent. Total population estimated at 30,000 pairs.

Index

Richards, A J
British birds.
1. Birds - Great Britain
I. Title
598.2'941   QL690.G7

ISBN 0-7153-7834-1

Photoset by
Advertiser Printers (Newton Abbot) Ltd.,
Devon
and printed in the Netherlands
by Smeets Offset B V Weert
for David & Charles (Publishers) Limited
Brunel House Newton Abbot Devon

Published in the United States of America
by David & Charles Inc
North Pomfret Vermont 05053 USA